S0-ATU-990

THE JAPAN THAT CAN SAY "NO"

—as excerpted from the *Congressional Record*

by
Akio Morita and Shintaro Ishihara

The Jefferson Educational Foundation
7414 Benjamin Franklin Station
Washington, D.C. 20044
1990

Printed in the United States of America.
First Edition.

Cover Photo: Jon Milburn

TABLE OF CONTENTS

FOREWORD

The material written in this book is a rough translation of the Japanese edition. There are obvious grammatical and punctual errors throughout the book and we apologize for this—as this is the best translation, in English, we could get.

THE NECESSITY FOR PRESENT DAY JAPANESE TO REFORM THEIR CONSCIOUSNESS

(ISHIHARA)

Japanese People Have Become Top Heavy

Each month, there is the Cabinet meeting for the economic report. I am one of those kinds of guys who gets up early and goes before the cabinet meeting, which winds up by 9 am, or 8 at the earliest. While rubbing my sleepy eyes, I go over the reports by the Bureau Chief of the Economic Planning Agency and by the Director of the Bank of Japan. Each month, the reports are almost identical. Generally, the Cabinet ministers sleep through it. When I suggested to the Chief Cabinet Secretary that in this age of governmental administrative reform, why not give up these meetings, the response, not entirely unexpected on my part, was that these were absolutely necessary, even if there were some Party executives who did not attend.

Thus, each month, there is repetition of a nearly identical report.

The Bureau Chief of the Economic Planning Agency said this month, just as he did last month, that the magnitude of Japan's surplus in international revenues was tending to shrink. In other words, this means he is saying that it is perfectly alright for business not to be so good. The Cabinet members all nod and underline this in red.

Myself, I thought this was a really strange phenomenon, so I turned to the Minister for Home Affairs, Mr.

1

Kajiyama, who was sitting beside me, and asked what was going on here. Everybody is thinking it's just great that business isn't prospering that much and eagerly red lining that information. Couldn't you say, however, that a country like that won't last long? Words, words—if the meaning of words keeps changing, you can never be really sure what is being said. In other words, aren't our values changing?

If we take Japan's vast trade surpluses as one type of crisis situation, then this points to the necessity of changing Japan's economic and industrial structure. While leaving undetermined for the moment of whether or not the conclusions of the Maekawa Report were valid, it is true that the "comprehensive and vast" industries are tending to recede and the lean and mean knowledge-intensive types are coming into their own. When the term "comprehensive and vast" [jukochodal] is applied to human beings, it is a form of praise, while the opposite, "light and small" would be to berate the same. However, when these terms are applied to the industrial structure, their meaning has come to change.

What matters, however, is whether or not this is good. Should we all be at ease, not that we are not dirtying our hands and sweating in order to make things with our own hands? Certainly know how comes about from one type of mental activity, and coming up with it is work worthy of respect. Looking at history, however, in cases where the whole society of the country was using their brains instead of their hands, not one has lasted to prosper today. In some sense, it may be true that the Japanese people are being forced into a new historical experience, but can we go on now, as we are, thinking we are the chosen people?

When looking at the actions of the Japanese people these days, I recall that these seem similar to ET, the extra-terrestrial, in the Spielberg films. I feel that it may well be the Japanese people will evolve into something like ET with pronounced eyes and noses and a big head making them top-heavy, over an abnormally thin body and slender arms and legs.

Therefore, it was impossible for Japan to get more than a few gold medals as the Seoul Olympics, which many Japanese read as being abnormal. While it may be that this is a sign that a new people has arisen to make contributions in other areas, it seems more natural to me that our descendants would be able to continue to sweat and work to keep the country strong.

Japan's Advanced Technology Is at the Heart of Military Strength

This is something advocated by Mr. Morita, who is a company leader that has driven Japan's advanced technology and who is known for manufacturing excellent products. He pointed out that the INF limitations (the restrictions on intermediate range nuclear forces) were something that the Soviet and American leaders came to each other on. While this was an epoch-making event, it was certainly not done because Americans and Russians had a new sense of the danger of nuclear weapons, they were not acting from the standpoint of human morality.

There may be some people who took the INF negotiations as a sign that both countries were beginning to act from their sense of humanity, but I think the reason why they got together on this is different.

Whether it be mid-range nuclear weapons or intercontinental ballistic missiles, what ensures the accuracy of weapons is none other than compact, high precision computers. As everyone knows, current ICBMs use the MIRV concept where there are multiple warheads. When an attacking missile gets near enough to be detected, the warhead splits into 8 or 9 separate heads. Not all of them contain hydrogen bombs, however, some are dummies designed just to dupe the enemy.

The remaining warheads lose speed, reenter from space, fall, run sideways and follow complicated paths, but in the end, they hit the targets picked for them by spy satellites and destroy them to within 1 second of latitudinal and longitudinal accuracy. For a Soviet ICBM, this would mean hitting the silo containing the retaliatory ICBM in Vandenburg AFB California.

These silos go 50 to 60 meters underground and are strong fortresses having thick walls of reinforced concrete. If a direct hit is not scored upon them, one cannot destroy the hydrogen bombs inside. The equipment will not even be affected as much as it is in an earthquake if a direct hit is not made. Thus, it is absolutely vital that a direct hit is made.

At the present time, Soviet technology allows these missiles to hit within a 60 meter accuracy, while for the U.S., it is 15 meters, and there is concern that this 15 meters has to be brought down to zero. This type of precision calls for a more complex orbit the further the attack proceeds, and only artificial intelligence can ensure accuracy. It may well be that America was the 4th generation leader and that the 1 megabit and several megabit devices which will support the next, the 5th generation, can be developed by American know how. However, to use this know how across diverse applications, including weapons, requires a country with dramatically advanced production management; it is only Japan that can deliver on it.

In sum, if Japanese semiconductors are not used, this accuracy cannot be assured. It has come to the point that no matter how much they continue military expansion, if Japan stopped selling them the chips, there would be nothing more they could do.

If, for example, Japan sold chips to the Soviet Union and stopped selling them to the U.S., this would upset the entire military balance. Some Americans say that if Japan were thinking of doing that, it would be occupied. Certainly, this is an age where things could come to that. The more technology advances, the more the U.S. and the Soviet Union will become dependent upon the initiative of the Japanese people—this is getting crazy now, but the point is clear.

The U.S. Defense Department's Science Commission recently prepared a huge classified report on electronic engineering. Looking at this, one can well understand the sense of crisis that the U.S. has with respect to Japan.

The report states that if Japan is left to go as it is, it will be impossible to get the lead back. This report is very accurate in assessing the areas of weakness in the U.S. and the strengths in Japan, but only the President and a few select people have seen the report. If it were seen by the general public, it would certainly raise quite a commotion. It is in this area where U.S. specialists have their greatest sense of danger, primarily centering on Japan's semiconductor technology.

—We have grown very dependent upon America's technological superiority in military strength. In that technology, electronic equipment is the most effective technology. Semiconductors are the "key" to preserving this superiority in electronic equipment, they are the "heart of the equipment." If competitive, mass production of semiconductors is the key, then this is in turn dependent upon having the market to support mass production.—

This dependence on the market for supporting mass production can be seen in that America did not have the vast and diverse needs for semiconductors, as Japan did in rice cookers and other household appliances. In Japan, these sizable and diverse needs created the market for semiconductor production. The report continues:

—America's Semiconductor Industry for its commercial mass production is losing its superiority minute by minute. There is a strong relationship between superiority in production technology and superiority in semiconductor technology, this is being transferred to foreign countries minute by minute. Very soon now, the defense of America will become dependent upon supply sources abroad. It is the opinion of the task team that this is something which is absolutely unacceptable for the United States—

What is meant in the report by "foreign supply sources" is none other than Japan. Further, they seem to worry about the following:

—What is more problematic is that electronic equipment systems are being transferred abroad, where they could more easily get transferred into the hands of the Soviet Union.—

In other words, their sense of crisis stems from the fact that semiconductor technology is absolutely vital in maintaining military superiority, and that this might flow from Japan to the Soviet Union. I feel that what is behind this abnormal hysteria on the part of this country is that this pivotal military technology is in the hands of another country, not even Europe, but in the hands of an Asian country, Japan.

Toshiba, etc. which was speared by COCOM is the fault of this hysteria by the U.S. If that had been criticism from the pure perspective of law, it would not for a moment have any basis at all.

The 1 megabit semiconductors which are used in the hearts of computers, which carry hundreds of millions of circuits in an area which is one-third the size of your little fingernail, are only made in Japan. Japan has nearly a 100 percent share of these 1 megabit semiconductors.

The United States has the know how to make them, but when it comes down to actual production, they don't have the technicians; they don't have the employees. Further, they don't have the production management.

Because they don't have development and production linked into one unit, they guard know how like a jewel.

America went after cheap labor and set up factories in Southeast Asia, where they could make 256k chips (¼ the capacity of 1 megabit chips), but they could not catch Japan. Now, Japan is at least 5 years ahead of the U.S. in this area and the gap is widening. There are even some kinds of basic research which cannot be accomplished without using one of these advanced computers. It takes excellent computers in order to develop other advanced computers—it is a cycle of technology. In other words, the bigger the gap in advanced computer technology, the more difficult it is to catch up.

The current situation in the world is that those kinds of computers are central to military strength and therefore central to national power. This is why the U.S. is being driven so hard. For example, in performing simulations of what elements would be needed by aircraft flying at mach 2, a regular computer might take 40 years to perform the necessary computations. If the same query is put to a new, advanced computer, however, the answer will come out in a year. Japan has almost the total share of the 1 megabit chips which are at the heart of these computers. In that sense, Japan has become a very important country.

There Is a Need for Japanese To Change Their Consciousness in Light of High Technology

As the world goes smaller, and issues in the world further settle down, whether it be China or Siberia, development will proceed. In order to get the needed access (participation in the market) the most important possibility lies in linear technology. Japan and West Germany are the most advanced countries in this research and development, and the theoretical base of Japanese technology is far superior. West Germany has given up in research on superconducting, but Japan has cleared the three technological obstacles which were envisioned by West Germany.

To make a long story short, the West German magnetic floating train development realized a levitation of only 8 mm, but Japan's "Maglevel" superconducting linear motorcar realized a levitation of 10 centimeters, and speeds of 500 kilometers per hour. This type of technology does not exist anywhere in the Soviet Union or the United States, it only exists in Japan and West Germany. If the giants in the economic field and the politicians can join together around this type of technology, it would open up new possibilities for our advancement. Whether or not this can be achieved depends upon our large and small choices in the future; in sum, it is a question involving the sensibilities of our politicians.

There is a Jiyu Shakai Kenkyu-kai (Free Society Research Association) which is presided over by Mr. Morita. This was formed more than 10 years ago as an association of politicians and businessmen. I am the youngest, but I also participate. We get together for discussions once or twice a year.

Recently, Mr. Kissinger predicted that Japan might become a military superpower. This, however, was not the foolish step of Japan getting ICBMs and refurbishing the old Yamato battleship, it pointed to the danger that no matter how much the U.S. or the Soviet Union developed space, equipped themselves with space platform weapons, the military initiative to control these would be dependent upon Japanese technology. The question now is whether Japan has politicians who accurately understand the history behind what we have now become.

We Japanese now face choices on whether we can boldly proceed or stand back quietly. It may be possible that Japan can secure a new culture for itself based upon the skeleton of the development of high level technology. We must not restrain ourselves to what we have done up to this point. The tax reform was one thing, we must boldly proceed in making a number of reforms. The dregs of the postwar period are too prominent in the consciousness of Japanese. I feel that however hesitatingly, the revolution in our consciousness has already begun.

The Soviet Union implemented a revolution in consciousness with its criticism of Stalinism, and China achieved the Great Cultural Revolution. The United States also realized a type of consciousness reform through its bitter experiences in the Vietnam War. Japan is the only one which has not felt the need for some kind of reform since the end of the war. We do not need a drastic reform of consciousness, but rather a smooth reform based upon the technology that we have developed for ourselves. I think that only by doing this will we realize a society which is mature in the true sense of the word.

THE DECLINE OF AN AMERICA WHICH CAN ONLY SEE 10 MINUTES AHEAD

(MORITA)

America Neglects the Significance of Production

The gist of the Ishihara message is the importance of production activities.

I have had frequent occasion to deliver speeches, both in Europe and in the United States, due to the nature of my business activities, and have involved myself in many debates at international conferences. As a result of my conversations with Europeans and Americans, I have become very aware of and concerned about the fact that they appear to have forgotten the importance of production activities.

Americans make money by playing "money games," namely, M&A (mergers and acquisitions), by simply moving money back and forth. If you look at the exchange rate, for example, the dollar is now worth about 120 Japanese yen, and enormous and quick profits are made by just moving money by computer, satellite and even by telephone.

The summer before last, I had the opportunity to talk to a group of three thousand foreign currency dealers, who specialize in buying and selling money, at a conference on the future of money transfers and finance. I have been known to be critical of the floating exchange rate system. Talking to money dealers about my ideas was like telling stockbrokers that the movement of stock prices is wrong; it takes a lot of courage. I stressed that

11

money should not be the subject of speculation, because the fundamental function of money should not be to enrich banks and security companies but to smooth the path of production activities. It has been said that America is entering a so-called post-industrial society where the weight of the service industry sector is growing. Yet, when people forget how to produce goods, and that appears to be the case in America, they will not be able to supply themselves even with their most basic needs.

Last summer, a friend of mine who is always criticizing Japan for being "unfair" invited me to his summer home to play golf. At the first tee, I pulled out my MacGregor driver whereas my friend had a Japanese Yonex club. I criticized him for using Japanese clubs since he had been telling everyone not to buy Japanese products. He responded simply, "These clubs give me better distance." Well, I was not able to convince him to sacrifice distance and so I kept quiet. After the game, he invited me to his house and while his wife was preparing dinner, he showed me around. In the garage, I saw a Kawasaki snowmobile, which he said he needed because winters in the northern part of New York State have a lot of snow. Next to it was a Japanese motor boat, which he said he needs because his house is surrounded by lakes. I also saw an off-road vehicle made in Japan.

Finally, dinner was ready and as I went into the house, I saw a Sony television and numerous other Japanese-made products. I said "You criticize us all the time for not buying American products while it's obvious that you prefer Japanese products. Are you asking us to buy something you won't buy yourself?"

Americans today make money by "handling" money and shuffling it around, instead of creating and producing goods and with some actual value.

America Looks 10 Minutes Ahead; Japan Looks 10 Years

I delivered a speech in Chicago entitled "Ten Minutes vs. Ten Years." I stated that we Japanese plan and develop our business strategies ten years ahead. When I asked an American money trader "how far ahead do you plan . . . one week?" The reply was "no, no . . . ten minutes." He was moving money through a computer, targeting the fate of that transaction ten minutes later. So, as I told the Americans, we are focusing on business ten years in advance, while you seem to be concerned only with profits ten minutes from now. At that rate, you may well never to able to compete with us.

A well-known economist, Peter Drucker, wrote recently; "Americans cannot live in a symbol economy where businessmen play only with numbers; Americans should come back to a real economy where money moves in accordance with real production activities."

Unfortunately, in America, stocks are owned and handled by institutional investors whose fund managers actually buy and sell stocks in huge numbers in an attempt to maximize profits in a given short period of time. At the slightest increase in stock prices, they sell, and when the profit margin of any company declines as a result of poor management, they sell before the company's stock prices begin to decline. For them, the name of the game is nothing but quick profits.

It is expected that the American service industry will flourish. This includes finance and financial services, where entrepreneurs and investors alike do not leave their money in long term projects, such as the ten-year projects that have been implemented in Japan. The American economy is, then, an economy without substance. It must return to a real production economy.

In America, R&D is closely linked to the military budget. R&D in the private sector is heavily dependent on military expenditure. As a result, a corporation can engage in the development of a new fighter without worrying about profit or loss. On the other hand, budget constraints on NASA and the military agencies will directly reduce the volume of R&D.

A ten-minute profit cycle economy does not permit companies to invest in long term development. There are some exceptions, such as IBM, AT&T, DuPont and some others. But they do not represent the mainstream of American business nowadays. Gradually but surely, American business is shifting toward a symbol economy. In addition, it seems fashionable to call the service industry the "futuristic third wave" and information and intelligence is the business of the future. But these produce nothing. Business, in my mind, is nothing but "value added;" we must add value and wisdom to things and this is what America seems to have forgotten. And this is the most deplorable aspect of America today.

Japan will do fine as long as it continues to develop

and produce things of tangible value; a shift from high technology industry to quick profits from the money game will only serve to accelerate the degeneration of the country. We must take precautions against such developments, providing for, for example, tax advantages for long term investments.

It is even more the case in America. A quick profit from a stock deal should be taxed at a higher rate than those on long term investment. Capital gains should be subject to a lower rate of taxation.

Recently I said, "America is supposedly the number one industrial country in the world. Why don't you have a Department of Industry?" Seated next to me was the chairman of Ford Motor Corporation, Mr. Caldwell, who replied "that's right—we are supervised by the Department of Transportation." The Department of Transportation is interested in emission control and highway safety, but has no interest in or jurisdiction over the future of the automobile industry in the United States.

America is the only nation among the advanced industrial countries that does not have a Department of Industry which is responsible for industrial policy. Instead, the Department of Commerce and USTR preside and their only real concern is trade related matters and the criticize others for the failure of American industry.

Japan's Impact on the World Economy Will Be Recognized

The American economy appears to be deteriorating. I assume that the Bush Administration will take steps to tackle the present problems, but the country as a whole seems to be extremely nonchalant about the so-called twin deficits: budget and trade.

There seems to be the feeling that Reaganomics raised the standard of living, taxes are relatively low, and they can buy goods from all over the world. When the Republicans captured the White House again, I began to wonder if there was any sector in America which was truly concerned about the twin deficits since Bush repeatedly denies any possibility of a tax increase. How in the world do the Americans expect to restore their economy?

Let's examine the price of gasoline. Consumption of gasoline is growing rapidly, yet the price is still below a dollar a gallon. The ongoing world price per gallon is $4 US. A one-cent per gallon tax-increase means an additional $10 billion; think what the government could get if they levied an additional 25 cents per gallon. Yet the government will not even begin to initiate such a move.

In fact, even with such an additional tax, American gasoline prices will still remain less than international prices. Politicians are simply afraid of losing votes by adopting unpopular policies. Some of my closest American friends have said that Bush could have been elected without promising not to raise taxes. He has so firmly committed himself and his administration to not raising taxes, yet it is so obvious that the twin deficits cannot be solved without additional national revenue.

Bush should have been more realistic if he was, and is, honestly concerned with the American budget crisis.

Tactically, he could have said early on that he would not raise taxes, but as he gained support, he should have become more honest and direct, and told the people that it was necessary to pursue a more realistic financial policy. On the contrary, he confirmed his pledge after he was elected. Solutions to the deficit problem seem even more remote.

This being the case, the US dollar has continued to decline, and the US has had to increase interest rates to further attract foreign money to the US, for which it will have to pay a great deal of interest. The result is an increasingly vicious circle.

The US inflation situation might well become an even more chronic phenomenon. Economic growth without inflation is ideal, whereas endless inflation might well bring the dollar's value to the level of trash. This, in turn, will make European and Japanese assets trash since sizeable assets of both are in US dollars.

Both the Europeans and Japanese cannot sit idly by, ignoring or overlooking the trend in the American economy. At one time, when the US dollar was very high, the Japanese and Europeans asked Americans if "they could absorb the trade deficit caused by the high dollar?" At that time, Treasury Secretary Regan was of the opinion that the US dollar should stay high and strong. When James Baker became the new Secretary of the Treasury, he recognized the problem and entered into the Plaza Accord to lower the value of the dollar.

The American economy does not stand alone. It is not only a domestic issue. The collapse of the American economy would cause a worldwide disaster. 1987's

Black Monday chilled all nations momentarily. I am not a pessimist, but I cannot help thinking that unless the Bush Administration handles economic issues very seriously, a worldwide collapse is not just a worry, but a very real possibility. The ever-growing American inflation and this economic crisis will not only make other nations catch cold, but bring their economies into crisis as well.

It is said that Japan contributed to efforts to stop a possible disastrous chain reaction ignited by Black Monday which began in America and soon affected the London stock market as well. At that point, the Japanese Ministry of Finance asked Japanese institutional investors to support prices for a time, which instantly normalized Japanese stock prices. Later, the chairmen of one of the major US banks, who was visiting Japan, told me "it was Japan who put a stop to the chain reaction, and it was the Ministry of Finance who was able to move the Tokyo stock market. The Japanese government now has the clout to sustain Wall Street and the City of London. So-called Japanese guidance is truly powerful."

This gentleman went on to say "we are worried about the fact that the Japanese people are unaware of the fact that they have a significant impact on the world economy. And I believe it is true that Japan's economic status has been much enhanced.

Like it or not, this is the picture held by Americans, and the Japanese people have to recognize it and, inevitably, they have to behave in accordance with that status in the world community today.

RACIAL PREJUDICE IS AT THE ROOT OF JAPAN BASHING
(ISHIHARA)

America Will Never Hold Its World Leadership
Position Unless It Ends Its Racial Prejudice

I had the opportunity to visit Washington, D.C. in April a year ago, and was surprised at the very hostile atmosphere. It was only five days after Congress passed the resolution condemning Japan on the semiconductor issue. I met some of my old friends, senators and congressmen, who with subtle smiles admitted that racial considerations or more directly, racial prejudice, played a role in US–Japan relations. This was after I had discussed several concrete examples with them. Although they shied away from the subject of racial prejudice as if it were taboo, they did admit that it is there.

Initially, they violently denied my allegations, citing that the Pacific War of 40-some years ago as the only real source of prejudice against the Japanese. I declared that it was not as simple as that. It appears that the Americans were firmly of the opinion that is was the West, namely Euro-Americans, who established modernism. My reaction was as follows.

It may be true that the modern era is a creation of the white race, but you have become somewhat presumptuous about it. In the pre-modern era, Asiatic races such as Genghis Khan and his armies raided the European continent, destroying towns and villages, looting and raping. Yet at that time, many Europeans actually imitated the style and behavior of Khan's hordes, cutting their hair short, shaving their eyebrows, and walking menacingly with knees apart. That was nothing compared to the strange ways modern Europeans and Americans adopt the style and fashions of some of the present era's heros, such as the Beatles and Michael Jackson. Even Asian kids do this. Probably Khan was some kind of cult figure then and white women regarded him as a "hero" of sorts.

Some say that the roots of the so-called "yellow peril" can be traced back to atrocities committed by Khan and his men. At any rate, we should keep in mind that there is prejudice against Orientals, as the following episode illustrates.

I had the chance to talk with the Secretary of the Navy about the Amber System. Amber is supposed to be the color of caution and danger and this system is named for this concept. Under the Amber System, ordinary vessels such as tankers and container ships, are equipped with sonar on their bows. The sonar can detect underwater objects. Some objects are rocks, etc., which navigational charts will show. What the system is looking for are nuclear submarines.

The Amber System alone cannot detect the nationality of the submarines detected; it cannot tell if they are American, Russian or whatever. It simply detects the presence of some foreign object and this information is relayed directly to the Pentagon, which knows what is on the navigational charts and also where U.S. subs are located, so they will be able to ascertain whether the particular sub is American or not.

I suggested that the Navy equip all Japanese commercial vessels with this system. Japanese seamen are reliable and the Japanese merchant marine travels all the oceans and seas. Japanese vessels, including our oil tankers, could gather information along vital cargo routes and the U.S. could analyze the information received from the Japanese ships.

To my surprise, the Americans said that it was none of Japan's business. I asked that how, in light of the very limited number of U.S. ships, can you deny the need for such assistance. The answer, "We cannot leave such a critical matter with Japan." I asked if it was appropriate to involve the British and Germans, and they said it would be.

The fact of the matter is that Americans do not trust Japan. Japan would have no basis with which to analyze the information collected by the Amber System, yet they still worried about the Japanese reliability in merely collecting the information. It seems that in their minds, even the Soviets are more trustworthy than the Japanese. American racial prejudice toward Japan is very fundamental and we should always keep it in mind when dealing with the Americans.

During the Second World War, Americans bombed civilian targets in Germany, but only on Japan did they use the atomic bomb. While they refuse to admit it, the only reason they could use the atomic bomb on Japan was because of their racial attitude toward Japan. The fact that they actually dropped the atomic bomb on Japan is sufficient indication that racial prejudice was a factor.

It is my firm conviction that the roots of the US–Japan friction lie in the soil of racial prejudice. American racial prejudice is based upon the cultural belief that the modern era is the creation of the white race, including Americans. This confidence appears a bit overwhelming, probably due to America's relative youth as a nation, which tends to blind it to other cultures. If Americans were ever to be made aware of the presence of a real Japanese culture in the Azuchi-Momoyama period as did the Spanish and Portuguese missionaries, they may develop some respect for Japanese cultural history. Unfortunately, the present American education system does not teach children the value of other cultures. In the period noted above, there were over 20,000 "terakoya" schools all over Japan. No other nation had such an extensive schooling system at such an early point in their history.

During the Edo period, even farmers and peasants were able to read and write at least one or two thousand characters, including hiragana and katakana. Japan already, at that time, had a complete postal network, called "hikyaku" as far as the southernmost end of Kyushu. Documents and information of various kinds were available in libraries in many cities and towns.

This is the kind of information I give to Americans who exhibit ignorance of our culture. Unfortunately, most Americans don't like to see these facts, and they tend to change the subject. In short, their historical prejudice and cultural narrowness has reached a point where they cannot see another's point or see the value of another culture. All this has made Americans, in the post war period, very irritable on the issue.

The American position at this point seems to be that

the British and Germans can play whatever role the Japanese could, and can do so without irritating the U.S. Americans are essentially an honest people, and in fact do admit to the existence of racial prejudice, if they are pressed on the subject, which I do. However, this is not enough. They should also admit that prejudice does not hold any solutions to the problems developing in the world today. It is important that they face the situation aware of the historical context, seeing that the reality is that the power in the world, including economic power, is shifting gradually from West to East. I may not be as strong a shift as is expressed in the "Pacific era," but at any rate it is in America's interest to rid itself of prejudice against Asia, including that against Japan, in order to maintain a position of leadership in the world.

Japan Should Become More Cosmopolitan

The calendar clearly indicates that we are moving toward the end of a century, and with it is coming the end of the modern era as developed by white Westerners. History is entering a period of new genesis. The promoter of this new era is Japan as well as the U.S. It is a political development which America's political leaders should make known, so that America will be better equipped to meet the tasks of the future.

The Japanese have their own problems. They may have to go through a mental evolution to meet the needs of this new era. As Mr. Morita has pride and confidence in the products of his company, an attitude which has made him a truly cosmopolitan man, so must the Japanese develop pride and confidence in our culture and our technology. We cannot become overbearing, which will not be tolerated in the new era, but by the same token, an inferiority complex is equally harmful. The Japanese people must move out of their current mental stagnation; I feel this is especially important for Japanese diplomats.

Except for the young and the especially qualified, most Japanese diplomats suffer from a peculiar inferiority complex and as a result are spreading the seeds of misunderstanding throughout the world. When I was young, I had the opportunity to live with one of Japan's ambassadors and his family. He was a hell of a nice guy—a really wonderful human being. However, he seldom socialized with anyone. At the end of a game of golf, if someone suggested dropping into the lounge for a beer, he would refuse saying that he preferred to have one when he got home. This is the same attitude that some Japanese have when they won't even accept a cup of tea while a guest in another's home. It may be for most Japanese that only in his home and only with his family can he really relax. If this is true, then the Japanese can never be truly cosmopolitan. When the heads of some of Japan's top trading companies, such as Mitsubishi and Mitsui, wanted to join prestigious country clubs in the countries in which they were stationed, their applications were rejected because it was felt that Japanese were too parochial, staying to themselves and not socializing with others. Some Japanese diplomats don't hesitate to show their inferiority complex. One ambassador even publicly said that the Japanese were a race of "pygmies." Such things happen all the time!

The Ministry of Foreign Affairs tried to cover up the news of the firing training by an American cruiser (the Towers, 3370 tons) last year in Tokyo Bay. A single cannon on the Towers, the Mark 42, can send a 32 kg ball over 23 kilometers at 36 rounds per minute. Americans authorities said non-explosive training ammunition was being used. But even these could easily damage of Uraga class Japanese Coast Guard frigate (33231 tons), not to mention what it could do to small fishing vessels. Tokyo Bay is a busy commercial harbor, similar to New York Harbor, inside the Verranzano Bridge. American television reported that the American people would be furious if that happened in their country.

The Ministry of Foreign Affairs asked the Japanese media to hold the story until further notice, since that event was incidental. I was very angry and protested, saying that I would release the news on my own. This happened on Japanese sovereign territory in an area clearly barred from such firings due to the fact it was a vital maritime channel. It was a clear violation of Japan's sovereign rights. I observed that "it was like seeing a ranking Self Defense Agency official firing his service revolver at the Ginza junction." I still feel the same way.

Americans can say that they are here to protect Japan under the US–Japan Security Treaty. But at times, it appears to me that the Americans behave more like mad dogs instead of watch dogs.

I use the term "mad dogs" when referring to the Americans recalling that Mr. Shiina, Deputy President of the LDP, used it when he was Foreign Minister. This is another instance where "no" clearly said when that is what he meant would be useful. One must say "no" when he means "no" and failure to do so reduces credibility. In the case of the US–Japan relationship, such an attitude only further increases Americans racial prejudice. The Japanese people should know that they are in essence protecting American interests as the new era in international relations begins, something the Americans seem quicker to sense. This is the reality of the US–Japan relationship today.

BASHING JAPAN GETS VOTES
(MORITA)

*The Paradox of Welcoming Investment but Criticism
of Japan*

I am worried about the tide of attitude in America
with respect to Japan.

The U.S. government and the Congress have adopted
a number of harsh policies with respect to Japan. Some
37 states in the U.S. have established offices in Tokyo.
Since I am responsible for investment-related matters in
the Keidanren [Federation of Economic Organizations],
when the state governors visit, I am the one to meet
with them if my time permits.

It never fails, they are always coming to Japan saying
"invest, please invest." Just when I am about to assume
that America welcomes Japanese, U.S. congressmen
elected from these same states are bashing Japan. The
state government has no involvement with this, of
course, but they are saying to Japan's big business,
"come on, come on."

"What in the world is the meaning of this?" I wonder.
In addition, recently a number of famous academics and
journalists have published books which are critical of
Japan. Recently, there has been a book, "Buying into
America" which suggests that Japan is buying up
America, and there is a book called "Yen" which envi-
sions a future after the year 2000 in which Japan uses
its financial power to control the world. The latter is
rather calm in its perspective, but both books reveal a

27

clear Japanese menace—the tides have really shifted since "Japan As Number One" was published.

A book written by a famous journalist which depicts Japan in a very harsh light has become a best seller, so this is indicative of the critical attitude on Japan held by the American masses. The more this attitude increases, politicians will beat up on Japan in an attempt to make votes for themselves, because getting votes is the most important aspect of being a politician.

The politicians themselves are not at all concerned, however. When asked why they bash Japan, they respond that if they say "Japan is good," votes will drop off. If Japan is bashed, further, if a Toshiba radio-cassette player is smashed, this is not indicative of hating Toshiba, but they think if they do such things, votes will increase.

The state governments welcome Japanese industry because if they invest in their state, tax collections increase along with employment, but among the American people, the attitude with respect to Japan is becoming more and more critical.

The Keidanren has established a "Council for Better Investment in the United States," which is the English language name of the council (literally it is the "Council for Investment in the U.S.—translator). What we mean by "better investment" is the type of investment which will get Americans on Japan's side. If the number of Americans view things the way Japan does increases, then bashing Japan will cause lower vote counts. That would probably make politicians stop bashing Japan.

I think that it is vital that we help build a feeling of

friendship among the American masses with respect to Japan. At the present time, everyone buys Japanese goods and is delighted with them. They do not hate Japanese products. What makes them hate Japan, however, is that when Japanese businesses enter the American society, they have the feeling that foreigners are coming.

Japanese Industries in the U.S. Should Work at Community Service

Direct investment in the United States is currently expanding very rapidly. The end result of this is that Japanese companies, including Sony, have established themselves in local districts throughout the country. When the English or French invest in a local area, the communities and local society do not see this as an invasion of foreigners. However, when the Japanese come, they feel that strangers, or something foreign has entered their midst. This gives them strong feelings of fear and anxiety.

To give a simple example, when Japanese go to the U.S., their children go to the schools. The schools have an organization, the P.T.A. This stands for Parent and Teachers Association. The corresponding organization in Japan is called the "Fathers and Brothers Association" but no fathers and brothers participate, it is more of a "mothers and sisters" association. Myself, I have never attended the Fathers and Brothers Association in Japan. In the case of Americans, however, husbands go with their wives to attend meetings for their elementary

school or local area school and discuss how those
schools should be run. In Japan, it is the mother's duty
to take care of educational matters for the children, so
the father does not attend. In America, however, when
the father takes off work to attend a PTA meeting, his
company does not charge him leave. The man, therefore,
must go to the PTA meetings.

When I was living in the U.S., I went to PTA meetings where I was able to associate with persons from
various walks of life. My daughter went to the Nightin-
gale Bonford School in Manhattan and my son went to
St. Bernards. I got to know Stokowski (the late) conduc-
tor at one of the PTA meetings. John Gunther, a very
influential behind-the-scenes man was also someone I
met through PTA, he is now the Ambassador to Austria.
Henry Grunwald, the editor of Time, was a classmate
of my daughter's who I also got to know.

At a gathering of Japanese businessmen in the United
States, I got up and told them "to go as a couple to the
PTA to get to know the other people involved and to
start getting personally involved in the school." The
people I was speaking to make such remarks as "I don't
like to hear that," or "Why do we have to do that."
When I told them there was actually a meeting the other
night and asked what they did, the responses were "I
was too busy. I sent my wife," or "My wife can't speak
English so she just gossiped with the other Japanese
women and came home." Because of instances like this,
there is no doubt that the PTA view them as the foreigners who'd come to town.

Also, when Sunday morning comes, the whole community dresses up and goes to church. At that time, however, the Japanese are all walking in the opposite direction to the country club. When they are asked why they are not going to church, they are likely to respond that "I'm a Buddhist," or a similar reply. I'm not saying that they should necessarily go to church, but it is natural for the people of the community to think that some really strange foreigners are in their midst when they see them all trotting off to the golf course on Sunday morning.

I golf in America too. But I always do it with foreigners. When Saturday night comes, I take my wife to the country club, have dinner and talk with the other members. However, golf for Japanese is usually a business-related event; there are usually guests from Japan and a group solely composed of Japanese people plays the course. This is another way in which a strange image is transmitted to the local community.

Another example is that American wives often volunteer their spare time for community service activities, such as preparing braille for the visually handicapped. Japanese housewives normally do not participate in such activities.

There are also public fund-raising dinner parties for local community centers, which does not involve mere contributions, it is a major social event where funds are raised. Tickets for the party are $30, $50, $100, and $300 which represent contributions for the fund raising event. They view participation in these events as a contribution to their local society. While this is a little different than the golf example above, it is another area where Japanese isolate themselves as strange foreigners.

It is vital that we participate in the local society in order to resolve any racial problems. When Japanese build factories in the United States, these usually go to the regional or rural areas due to the large amount of space they require. In such a small community context, if Japanese avoid contributing to the local community, they will be disliked in the area, and then the people of that area will cast their votes for Japan-bashing politicians.

One Japanese company that had established in the U.S. had its headquarters in Japan make a very substantial contribution to build a community center, in an effort to counter any adverse prejudice, even though the local company had not yet become profitable. The local community was delighted and named the hall after the company that had contributed. When the plant manager was reassigned back to Japan, the whole community threw a "sayonara" party for him.

I am not saying that all Japanese companies coming to the United States are bad, but just a little kindness and consideration can turn around attitudes about Japanese people. The Council for Better Investment in the United States is trying very hard to get this information out in an effort to have the Japanese company weave itself into the fabric of the local community in which it is locating.

At the current time, two hundred and forty or fifty companies who have invested in the U.S. are members of the Council, but it aims to attract even more members.

Information about these efforts is gradually becoming known in the U.S., and this has already done much to change perceptions there. I think Japanese people in the U.S. are also making better efforts.

Let's Build an American Society where Japan Bashing Causes Votes to Decline

Therefore, I think that the only way to erase the perception Mr. Ishihara points to where Japanese are disliked just for being Japanese is to make the above types of efforts. This is because they [Americans] are stubborn and are not likely to be induced by saying "you guys change."

I have so many American friends myself that I have been accused of being an American. Since I have lived in America and have been counted as a friend by many Americans, I am not overly sensitive to what is said about me. As Ishihara has said, to Americans; they feel that because their hair color is different, it is difficult for them to know what Japanese are thinking. I think there is another important point. The way of delivering a message is different. The structure of the Japanese language and English is different, and this affects our discussions together.

I have written this elsewhere in a book, but when Japanese read Chinese, they put in arrows and symbols to change word order, but Chinese read it directly and understand the meaning of the sentence immediately. English is the same kind of language, which is read one word after the other. In sum, this means that American have a different sequential order in thought processes. Therefore, no matter if you use interpreters, it is impos-

sible to interpret in the same sequential order as the
thought process that generated the words in Japanese.
Thus, when a message is to be delivered, it is regrettable
but true, that the sequential thought process of Japanese
is in the minority in the world. When communicating
with occidentals, who are in the majority, if things are
not communicated in an order they can comprehend,
they do not understand what we are saying. It is necessary that we be cognizant of this disadvantage that Japan
has in this area.

While the color of our hair will never be identical to
Americans, from the point of view of practical businessmen, I think we must recognize that if the current trade
imbalance with the U.S. is not rectified, America will
always say Japan is at fault. If Japanese business does
not go to the U.S. with manufacturing and sales to bring
down the imbalance, there is no way the problem will
be rectified. We must bring our factories to foreign
shores, and invest in these areas where our goods are
sold.

At this point, if there are any racial problems, it would
be the fault of the Americans, but that does nothing
to resolve them. Through the successes of Japanese-
American citizens groups, racial problems are not so
prominent anymore. When the Second World War began, all Japanese-Americans were places in detention
camps.

In the United States, people having different colored
skin have realized great successes. An example is the
Wang company which was founded by a Chinese. In
our quest to find why it is only Japan that is bashed,

it would be a bit strange to say it is because Japan is not internationalized, but it is really because we have been lax in not following the "when in Rome, do as the Romans do" in incorporating ourselves in the local community. I think this is why we remain foreign. That is exactly why I am saying we need to make such efforts. I am not saying that everything they do is alright, but I am saying there is a need for internationalization by both parties, and we have the need to do business.

The internment of Japanese-Americans during the war was a prime example of the emotionalism that the U.S. displayed with respect to Japan. After the passage of 40 years, the President has finally publicly recognized that this was wrong. It would be nice if emotionalism with respect to Japan ended right there, but that is not the case. An example is the Toshiba clause in the Omnibus Trade and Competitiveness Bill—no buying of Toshiba products—Toshiba Machine is bad.

I said in a speech that this was a violation of the U.S. constitution. This was due to the provision in the constitution which proscribes the enactment of laws which would deal retroactively with crimes. It also allows anyone accused of a crime the opportunity to defend himself. In the process of compiling this bill, sanctions were put on Toshiba for its crime. Toshiba had already been punished for its crime under Japanese law; but by adopting these sanctions restricting Toshiba's business activities, the Bill would impose retroactive punishment.

When I recently spoke in Seattle, I suggested that this Bill was unconstitutional, that it was an emotional response, and that it should be treated as an emotional international issue, which was similar in substance to the internment of Japanese-Americans during the war.

When something can become this emotional, perhaps Mr. Ishihara is right in his contention that racial problems lie at the root of the problem.

During the occupation era, the Americans built fences and stayed inside and didn't mingle too much with the Japanese people. This created an unpleasant atmosphere. Now, however, there are no occupation zones and we are at peace, we must behave appropriately and associate with each other.

If we do make efforts in the direction I have indicated to establish a framework where Japan bashing politicians are rewarded by fewer votes for their efforts, there is no doubt that political pressure will be exerted to the point where there can be no reduction in frictions between the countries.

Thus, it is my way of thinking that Japan must take the kind of action this situation calls for.

AMERICA ITSELF IS UNFAIR
(MORITA)

America Lacks Business Creativity

Americans and Europeans are always saying "We're getting ripped off by Japan. They take the ideas we have invented, make products and then the onslaught comes. We are being damaged, they're disgraceful." Japan has certainly done better more recently, but the U.S. and Europe are very much advanced in basic research.

Last year, I was invited to speak to about 100 researchers who worked at the Bell Laboratories at ATT.

The Bell Laboratories have about 7 people who have won the Nobel Prize. To me, it seemed that I would be speaking before some of the greatest men of our time. Prior to the speech, I was shown around the Bell Laboratories, where a number of wonderful research projects were underway.

As you must know, the transistor and the semiconductor, which are at the root of the current revolution in industry were invented at the Bell Laboratories. It really brought home to me how wonderful America was.

The basic message I brought that day was that this type of research was extremely significant academically in terms of both science and culture, but to be significant from the standpoint of business and industry, two other types of creativity, in addition to the creativity required to make the original invention, were absolutely necessary.

Industry requires three types of creativity. The first, of course, is the basic creativity necessary to make technological inventions and discoveries. This alone, however, does not make for good business or good industry.

The second type of creativity that is necessary is that involving how to use this new technology, and how to use it in large quantities and in a manner that is appropriate. In English, this would be called "product planning and production creativity."

The third type of creativity is in marketing. That is, selling the things you have produced. Even if you succeed in manufacturing something, it takes marketing to put that article into actual use before you have a business.

The strength in Japanese industry is in finding many ways to turn basic technology into products and using basic technology. In basic technology, it is true that Japan has relied on a number of foreign sources. Turning technology into products is where Japan is number 1 in the world.

Sony was the first company in Japan to license the transistor patent from Bell Laboratories, back in 1953. At that time, the transistor was only being used in hearing aids. We were repeatedly told to take this transistor and manufacture hearing aids.

When we brought this new transistor back to Japan, however, Mr. Ibuka, of Sony said, "There is not much potential in hearing aids, let's make a new transistor and build radios." At this point, we put all our energies each day in developing radios which used transistors. One of our researchers during this development effort, Mr. Esaki, subsequently went to work for IMB where he earned a Nobel Prize, but it was at our company where

he did work worthy of the Prize. There are a number
of Japanese who have received Nobel Prize, but Esaki
was the only one who worked for a research laboratory
of a company. We poured money into development of
new transistors, and developed small radios for the market, an effort that was worthy of the Nobel Prize.

It was an American company, however, who made
the first transistor radio. I became a salesman, and took
my product with full confidence to the United States to
sell it. Prior to this sales effort, the newest innovation
was a vacuum tube type of amplifier which required a
lot of space. When the American company, which was
a famous radio manufacturer, was initially rebuffed by
people telling him "since we have this great sound and
large speakers, who would want to buy your little radio,"
that company just quit trying to manufacture transistor
radios.

We, however, had something else in mind as a way
to sell these radios. "Currently in New York, there are
some 20 radio stations broadcasting 20 different programs during the same time frame. If everyone had their
own radio, then each person could tune in to the program
he or she wanted to listen to. Don't be satisfied with
one radio for the whole family, get your own radio. The
next step was to do the same for televisions." This was
a new marketing concept. One radio for one person
became a kind of catch phrase in this campaign and the
result was that Sony transistor radios became famous
throughout the world.

While it is true that Sony was second in developing
the transistor radio, the company who did it first lacked

the marketing creativity, so without much thought, they simply quit and pulled out of the market.

America has stopped manufacturing things, but this does not mean that they do not have the technology. The reason why the link between this technology and business has not been firmly connected is because they lack the second and third types of creativity, turning products made with the new technology into a business. I feel that this is a big problem for them. This exact area happens to be Japan's stronghold for the moment.

When I went to speak at Bell Laboratories, I got the chance to look at a lot of their research and advanced technology. I felt that they may well come up with something new that was even more important than the transistor, but since Bell Labs is a part of ATT, they are not thinking of anything except for telecommunications applications. There is not one person there who is thinking about how to use the new technology they are developing as a business. I think that this is one area where the U.S. comes up wanting. It is my feeling that even though times are good in America now and employment is up, the time will never again come when America will regain its strength in industry.

There is a television network in the U.S. called CBS. CBS has a weekly program which airs every Sunday evening called "60 Minutes," which has a very high viewership rating. This is a news program which devotes segments just under 20 minutes to various stories and opinion from around the whole world. More than 10 years ago, I was on the program. This is a program that takes a lot of money to produce. A crew followed me around Europe for about 6 months to prepare the segment.

Now they want me to do another one. A cameraman followed me to London, and when I went to Singapore, they followed me there too. The other day, a famous and beautiful interviewer in the U.S., Dianne Sawyer, came to Japan to interview me for the program. We spent a long time in front of the TV cameras, and the questions grew sharper. This made me mad and at the end, it was like we were in a fight.

She asked me what I thought of Lee Iacocca. Since this is a program he would be sure to see, I was frank in my statements. I said he was a disgrace, and that he was unfair. Iacocca comes to Japan and says Japanese are unfair. Very recently, he headed his sentence with "Let me make myself very clear," and then he went on to slander Japan. I know he wrote that book which labeled Japan as "unfair" but I think it is Iacocca who is unfair, and this is what I said.

When I was asked why he was unfair. I answered clearly, in front of the camera.

The president of a Chrysler company came to Japan. I had met this person before. I knew he was involved in selling Chrysler automobiles, so I asked him how sales were going. He turned to me and said quite plainly that he had not come to Japan to sell cars, but he had come to purchase Japanese parts and engines. He said he had come to Japan to buy Japanese products so they could sell them in the U.S.

At the present time, the three big automobile manufacturers have purchased 250,000 automobiles from Japan in 1987. How many have they sold to Japan? Only 4,000. They make no effort at all to sell their cars in Japan, and then call Japan unfair because Japan sells too much in the U.S. and that Japan will not buy their products.

One of the reasons why U.S.–Japan relations are in such a mess is that Japan has not told the U.S. the things that need to be said.

Japan Has Not Forced Its Sales on the U.S.

When I go to foreign countries, I hear that Japanese work too much. But why is working too hard so bad? Our society cannot continue to eat unless we keep producing products. People have to have products in order to live. They use golf clubs, and drive automobiles. If they want these products and do not wish to import them, they must manufacture them. I am a businessman. I am not forcing my customers to buy things from me. We expend our energies on how to make our products most attractive to the customer.

The Americans say that there is a U.S.–Japan trade imbalance, and it is not because Japan is not buying U.S. products or because Japan is forcibly selling the products. There are few things in the U.S. that Japanese want to buy, but there are a lot of things in Japan that Americans want to buy. This is at the root of the trade imbalance. The problem arises in that American politicians fail to understand this simple fact. It could never be the case that we are selling too much; it is not because we are exporting, the imbalance arises as a result of commercial transactions based on preferences.

Therefore, the only thing that Americans or Europeans can do to correct this imbalance is reassess themselves and make an effort to produce products which are attractive to Japanese consumers. It is in this area where I would like to see Japanese politicians get courage enough to expound abroad to our trading partners.

Recently, U.S. Secretary of Commerce Verity brought the representatives of 25 companies to Japan who wanted to sell their company's products in Japan. I was the person responsible for welcoming this group, and I told them that Japan would do its best to help out. I remarked, however, that I had been doing my best to sell Japanese products in the United States over the past 30 years. Yet, not once had the Minister of International Trade and Industry accompanied me and helped me out in my efforts. I asked the Secretary of Commerce if it was his intention to finally create an "America Incorporated." Secretary Verity smiled, but everyone else laughed out loud.

The Government of Japan has, in both the good sense and the bad sense, passed along various types of administrative guidance, which has been criticized by foreign countries as being an alliance between government and business—even if the Minister of International Trade and Industry does not go on trade missions.

One of the Americans in the group then asked me why the Japanese government backed up Japanese industry. Let's think about it. Even though the government does not own one share of my stock, I pay more than

half of my profits to the government in taxes. If my
business does not do well, the government does not
receive more revenues. Thus, the government, we feel,
is a kind of partner. I asked them why American industries which are paying taxes to the government say, "the
government is trying to control industry; don't touch
us." Your viewing of the government as the enemy
seems strange.

During this visit, Secretary Verity did voice his support for cooperation between government and business
to sell products, but it is my feeling that the establish-
ment of a framework for this type of cooperation is still
a long way off.

Let Us Think About the Role Japan Should Play in the World

On the other side of the question, however, there are
certainly aspects of Japan which are "unfair" when
viewed from the U.S. perspective. When you consider
what Japan has done for the world in the course of its
becoming the second largest economy, I think this is an
area where Japan is in line for some critical reflection.

Recently, since the time of Prime Minister Takeshita,
Japan has been making enormous efforts to become the
second most open country in the world for trading. The
long boiling problems over beef and citrus imports were
gradually resolved through efforts directed at these problems. However, from the perspective of Americans, Japan still has not done what it should do. I am not saying
we should put more money in defense spending, but if

we are not to exceed 1% of GNP on defense, then the government should put a lot more money into Official Development Assistance (ODA) (foreign aid), which helps the other countries of the world.

In addressing the ODA to GNP ratio, of the 18 countries in the world who provide foreign aid, Japan is number 15. Also, if we look at the amount of non-loan foreign aid for which there is no remuneration, Japan is number eighteen of eighteen. I shrink when I am asked whether that record is something Japan can be proud of.

Almost all U.S. corporations make donations of about 1 percent of their pre-tax profits to the community— using some of their money for the community is a kind of custom for them. In Japan, too, we also make some contributions to return money to society, and at the current time many Japanese companies are returning more than 1 percent.

But when Japan is looked at as a state, it is perceived as unfair by the rest of the world because it is not returning some of the benefits it reaps from the world back into the world society.

Therefore, when I speak before Japanese groups, I emphasize what is mean when America says Japan is acting disgracefully. I tell them, "Shouldn't we review what we are doing once again?" Japan should be bold in telling the U.S. what it needs to be told, but at the same time, Japan must establish a code of standards for the role it should be playing in the world.

Japan should open its markets to the extent where there would be no room for their complaints, and money that Japan has should be provided to help developing countries where people are not being oppressed. This would be a magnificent behavior on Japan's part, and I think that Japan needs to become aware of its responsibilities.

Certainly the full opening of our markets and advancing large sums of money for developing countries is very painful. However, things will not get better in the world until the pain is shared more equitably. How much pain do you think was involved during the Meiji Restoration where the privileged class of samurai gave up their power, cut their special hair styles, and tossed out their swords? It allowed a bloodless revolution to take place within Japan.

Mr. Ishihara has said there is a need for a reform of consciousness in Japan. He is exactly on the mark. If we do not reorient our consciousness from the perspective of being international people, then I do not feel Japan will be able to continue to walk the globe as an economic power.

THE CRITICISM OF JAPAN AS AN IMITATOR IS OFF THE MARK
(ISHIHARA)

The America Which Closes Its Eyes to Its Own Unfairness, and Criticizes Japan

The more I hear Americans bellowing complaints that Japan is unfair, the more I would like them to calm down and think. An example is a harsh exchange between myself and the U.S. Secretary of Commerce. It was a coincidence, but at a time when Commerce Secretary Verity visited Japan, there had been an agreement for an American company to participate in the second phase construction at Haneda International Airport. Verity was in Japan, and his mission included offering his thanks for this deal. However, I threw some cold water on him by saying that this would be the only time I would permit such a big commotion over such an issue.

The U.S. Congress had been criticizing Japan for having a "closed" market in large construction projects. In fact, however, there was only one U.S. construction firm that had been licensed to work in Japan—two, if you count pending applications. They say that the barriers are too thick, but I think that anyone wishing to do business in a foreign country has to make some adjustments to correspond to the local conditions.

After we went back and forth along that line, I commented that Japan's design for the Airport Building and the Shinkansen [bullet train] station, including the interior was poor—not refined enough and too idiosyncratic.

I went on to say that this might well be something which could be consigned to a foreign country.

This was true of Narita International Airport too. I noticed the other day that the pillars were painted with rust-proofing primer coat. When I suggested to the person in charge that he get busy and have them painted, he said, "Mr. Minister, did you just notice this? They have been that way since the airport was completed." When I asked why, he replied that it was OK this way because of the contrast between the red, white and black. When I asked whose design that was, he calmly replied that the painting contractor had made the determination.

Actually, there is not even a bar in the whole airport. One might like to have a drink to ease one's tension about flying before the flight, or one after to relax. Foreign airports always have a place where you can get a drink. Day or night, there is a place where the customer can get a drink. This is an integral part of air travel.

When I relayed these stories, Secretary Verity nodded his head, indicating that he understood my point. You could tell he was the Commerce Secretary, because when he went on to discuss the Kansai Airport, he said it would be a great idea if American companies could do the design.

Just that would be nice, he went on, but after it is completed, he said that the same number of U.S. aircraft should be permitted to fly from the airport as was permitted by Japanese carriers. I replied sharply, "No, that won't do." He turned colors and asked back, "Why not?"

There is an aviation treaty between the U.S. and
Japan. It is a relic of the occupation era. Not only is
it not balanced, it is outright unfair.

Among the mutually agreed upon rights in this treaty
is the right for air transport to points in the signatory
country, and for rights held unilaterally by the U.S.
side. America can fly into whatever Japanese airport it
pleases and then fly to anywhere else. In other words,
it has unlimited rights to fly through Japan to destinations
beyond.

Japan, however, only has the right to navigate through
limited airports, the economically unprofitable routes
from San Francisco–New York–Europe. Actually, these
routes are not even being used. During the U.S.–Japan
Summit in 1982, we were allowed two flights per week
from Los Angeles to Rio and San Paulo Brazil. One of
the concerns on the Japan side is that Nippon Cargo
Airlines (NCA) was finally obtaining 9 flights weekly
in 1985 on the Tokyo–San Francisco–New York route.

However, in exchange for this, America got the right
to land jumbo jets in Japan, and then fly from there
further in small cargo aircraft to Manila, Taiwan and
Korea. The most profitable rights went to the U.S. in
this agreement too. In the midst of all this, Japan cannot
get the right to fly a cargo aircraft in and out of Chicago.

While points of origin are limited by land space, Japan
is restricted to just three points, Tokyo, Nagoya, and
Osaka. America can fly to Japan from 19 airports. Looking at the number of flights, according to a study made
in November of 1988, Japan had 204.5 and the U.S.
371 passenger flights, and 60 cargo flights for Japan

versus 170 for the U.S. This is really unfair of the U.S. to be party to the U.S.–Japan Aviation Treaty which gives it so overwhelming of an advantage.

American specialists are well aware of this situation, so they do not want to engage in further negotiations. This type of situation continues while the U.S. makes selfish assertions.

I explained to the Secretary that since the U.S. maintained that attitude, it was at fault. The Secretary said he knew nothing of these matters. I pointed out to him that we couldn't even begin talking about getting negotiations started if he knew nothing about these matters.

An official from the State Department was accompanying the Secretary on his visit. He was an honest guy, and told the Secretary that the Treaty was indeed unfair. Secretary Verity became troubled. It was a very strange atmosphere between the Commerce Secretary and the official from the State Department, standing there in front of me, a Japanese. America is not the solid rock we thought it to be.

For example, relations are extremely poor between the Department of Commerce and the U.S. Trade Representative. Yeutter and Verity quarreled like dogs and monkeys, they never got along and were always bad mouthing each other. While none of these references about these two went on in front of me, there was an official from the U.S.T.R. in the delegation who was there to keep an eye on things.

Anyway, once the potential for a scene between the Secretary and me had quieted down, the "spy" from the U.S.T.R. caught my eye and said "Hang in there." I laughed, thinking what an interesting country the U.S. was.

Japan, A Country Where Each Person is Highly Creative

America closes its eyes to its own unfairness and criticizes others. I think that it should not be forgotten what such a shifty country has done.

As Mr. Morita has pointed out, it is off the mark to say that Japan has relied on the U.S. for the creativity to develop technology, and then has just cleverly developed and marketed it. Americans and Europeans say that Japan can do nothing but imitate, but it is not right for Japanese themselves to begin to agree with such a statement. The Japanese people have been possessed of creativity for ages.

There has been a gradual increase in the number of Americans and Europeans who recognize creativity in the Japanese. The same can be said for cultural creativity.

Take the field of literature. Some while ago, the French did not recognize Japanese literature at all. They did not think it had any value. More recently, however, the French have grown to appreciate Japanese literature more and more. The reason for this is quite interesting: it came about because of Japan's high technology. That is, foreigners who were interested in Japan's high technology began studying the Japanese language and started reading modern Japanese novels.

They recognized that modern Japanese literature was

indeed quite interesting. It was not their masters of literature or translators who pointed this out, but the intelligencia who were coming from scientific backgrounds.

In any case, I do not think we should stand still and agree that outside of literature, we are still nothing but imitators as the Americans say. It is time that Japanese take pride in their own spontaneous creativity and march forward.

Sony developed the transistor and took it to the U.S. market and changed the way Americans thought. In other words, they ripped apart the immutable principle of one radio per each family. The concept of making radios a personal appliance was nothing other than an exhibition of creativity on the order of that shown by Columbus.

The bountiful creativity of the Japanese is not something which can only be seen in a few of the elite, but something which can be broadly witnessed across the board in the general citizenry.

Japanese technology has found its way to the very heart of the world's military forces. I think this the product of the integration of our creativity.

Even if you have one creative genius, unless you can produce the product of his creativity in a factory, it will not come to anything. It takes a large number of excellent general technicians and excellent employees or one will not begin to see the light of day.

*The Excellence of Japanese Products Relates
to the Educational High Level of the Employees*

One can partially grasp the superiority of Japan's technological ability in the low rate of break down in Japanese products. The vital element in the excellence of technology and in tackling the problem of product break downs is possible because of the excellence in abilities of the general employees.

The U.S. Boeing Corporation which was scrutinized due to an aircraft crash was found to have problems with its employees' work methods, and they quickly set about making improvements. Certainly the re-education of the management could be undertaken quickly to the satisfaction of Japan and other countries, but since the level of the general employees was so low, concern remains in that area. When the president of Boeing's Seattle plant was asked: "How long will it take after re-education has begun before the technological strength [of your company] will begin bearing fruit?" His answer was seven years. Seven years! How can we ride around in jumbo jets for seven years not knowing what types of defects they might have?

As we learned from the tragic Boeing crash in Japan, all of those responsible got off, bearing no criminal responsibility. The legal systems in Japan and the U.S. are different; in Japan, a national inspector is sent out, but in America, aircraft manufacturers are not held responsible. The Boeing company did not even name the responsible persons. They say that it is better to prevent a recurrence then to spend all of their energies in finding fault, but the thinking that exemption from prosecution is the only way the truth can be told is something that is very hard to take for the families of those killed in the accident. According to an investigation by the Japanese police, there were four Boeing employees who should have been further pursued to assess their responsibility. The U.S. side acknowledges this.

The Boeing accident was nothing more than a worker's mistake—it happened well before the crash. There was no follow up after the crash except to say that the maintenance operations were sloppily done. While the specifications had called for three thick divider walls to be tightly bolted on, it just was not done.

Bolts had been placed on the left and right, but they did not reach through the three sheets, just to the second one. This caused a serious weakening of the aircraft strength. This tells the story of the low level of the people who are performing the maintenance.

Despite the fact that they are employees of the Boeing Corporation, a world-class manufacturer of aircraft, it would still take 7 years to re-educate them. This is a story which could not be comprehended in Japan's industrial circles.

The United States wants everyone to buy American-made semiconductors, and these are even being used in Japan, but the number of defective ones is amazingly high. When we complain, the answer is: Japan is the only country that is complaining, nobody else has any complaints. It leads me to think that there is no hope for the U.S.

The manufacturing defect rate in the United States

has improved somewhat recently, but it is still 5 to 6 times higher than that in Japan—it used to be 10 times higher. The report by the task team in the Pentagon also admits this.

To contrast this with Japan, I would like to insert the following episode.

This is an episode illustrating the exceptional knowledge and decision making capability of one female employee of the Kumamoto plant of Nippon Electric Corporation (NEC). For one reason or the other, the rate of rejects at the Kumamoto plant had been higher than it was at other NEC plants. No matter how hard they tried, they could not get the reject rate down. If it could be done in other plants, why couldn't it be done in Kumamoto? There were all-hands meetings with the plant supervisor daily on this problem.

One day, a female shift worker at the plant stopped at a crossing for the Kagoshima Line which ran in front of the factory. This was on her way to work. It was a rare event, but this day, she had to wait while a long freight train passed. Rumbling vibrations were sent through her legs as the train passed. The thought crossed her mind that these vibrations might have some sort of adverse effect on the products made at the plant. While she was working, she paid attention to the time and stopped when a train was scheduled to pass by. In the factory, however, she couldn't feel anything unusual. She still wondered, however, if the machines were not being affected. She reported her concerns to the foreman, suggesting that the precision machinery in the plant might be so affected.

The plant supervisor said, "That's it." He reacted immediately by digging a large ditch between the plant and the railroad tracks and filling it with water. The result was a drastic decline in the number of rejects.

That woman was 18 years old. This woman took pride in the products made by her company and identified with it. It is my feeling that this type of result is due to the vast differences in our formal education system.

In any case, when it comes to economics among the free world countries, the basis for existence is economic warfare, or, if that is too harsh a word, in economic competition. It is probably natural, therefore, that various cheerleading groups of the other party will rough you up by calling you unfair, but we cannot stand still and be defeated just because our adversary is making a lot of noise. This is exactly the position Japan is in today.

IS AMERICA A COUNTRY WHICH PROTECTS HUMAN RIGHTS?
(MORITA)

Workers' Rights Are Ignored by American Companies

American demands of Japan may increase in the future but America has a great many defects of its own, to which we must continuously direct its attention.

My long observation of American corporations leaves me puzzled about American human rights legitimacy. Human rights are held to be such high moral values in America and it preaches on the subject continuously all over the world. America has been criticizing and condemning nations such as South Africa and Afghanistan on human rights issues; however, I must ask Americans if they are applying these same standards to their own workers.

American corporations hire workers right and left and build new plants all over whenever the market is bullish, in an attempt to maximize their profits. Yet once the tide shifts, they lay off workers simply to protect company profits. These laid-off workers have nothing to do with poor market conditions.

American corporate executives are of the opinion that it is a corporate right to pursue maximum profits and that fired workers should be able to live on their savings. However, people do not work for wages alone. Work has more meaning to most people than just as a means of subsistence. A Japanese worker has a sense of mission in holding his job for his lifetime as well as supporting the corporation which provides him with meaning to his

life. This may well not be the case in America. American workers may only expect a comfortable wage for
their work. However, this attitude could change. People
can easily develop loyalty to a group or to a company
to which they belong depending upon conditions and
guidance provided. This sense of loyalty to the company
is a formidable asset. Repetitive hiring and firing denies
any possibility of cultivating a sense of loyalty.

I must ask American executives if they regard workers
as mere tools which they can use to assure profits and
then dump whenever the market sags. It seems that
workers are treated simply as resources or tools rather
than as human beings with inalienable rights. I would
like to suggest that they should first do something to
protect the human rights of workers in America before
they start asking other nations to protect and enhance
the human rights of their citizens. There are good reasons why American labor unions must be confrontational
in protecting their members and attempting to assure
maximum wages during periods of employment since
they have no assurance that the jobs will continue. Attitudes of executives are not actually much different than
those of the union to the extent that they grab whatever
they can–as much as half the company's annual profits
in the form of huge bonuses, claiming that this is just
since they were responsible for the profits.

A corporate chairman with whom I am acquainted,
complained that he has no use for all the money he
receives. His company is doing well and his income is
in the multi-million dollar a year range. His children are
all grown and he and his wife already have vacation

villas, a yacht and a private airplane; he said they just have no way to spend any more money on themselves.

Japanese executives work morning to night to improve the position of their companies, and yet the majority of their salaries are wiped out by taxes. The income gap between American and Japanese business executives is astounding. In Japan, even if one works very hard to increase his income to assure himself of some of the amenities of life, there is no way that he could expect to equal the luxuries enjoyed by American executives. Mr. Matsushita, probably the wealthiest man in Japan, when traveling abroad with his secretary, uses regular commercial flights. Having a private plane is simply out of his realm of consideration.

There is some talk in Japan concerning levying taxes on profits generated by the founder of a corporation. I am opposed to this proposal as I believe the spirit of free enterprise must be protected. While an unbridled pursuit of personal gain is not ideal, those who have created new business through extraordinary effort and who have made this contribution to society, should be rewarded financially to a certain extent as this will provide encouragement to young people, motivating them to follow their dreams and create new industries.

The current popular idea that everyone belongs in the middle class and the wealthy are suspect may undermine the very basis of a free economy. The Liberal Democratic Party, however, tends to accept this premise, as put forth by the opposition for the sole purpose of parliamentary manipulation, which is a shame since they have a 300-seat majority.

Japan has been a practicing free economy and a good majority of the people do in fact belong to the so-called middle class, which I think is marvelous. We have no real social classes and everyone is free to choose whatever profession or occupation they wish.

Today in Japan, nearly all company executives dine out on company accounts and ride in corporate-owned cars. As a child, I never saw this land of lavish living by corporate executives such as my father. He had a car and a chauffeur, but they were financed directly by him, out of his own pocket. It would be beyond his comprehension to use a company car and driver for his personal use. I am not particularly opposed to such benefits enjoyed by today's executives, as they can be correct rewards and incentives.

American corporate practices, from my personal observations, are extreme. An example is the so-called "golden parachute" which is the ultimate executive privilege. When ones reputation as an executive is well established and he is hired by another company, his contract may well contain these "golden parachutes." The executive may demand a certain percentage of corporate profits as his bonus, or perhaps some stock options. Upon retirement, he may still receive his salary for a number of years. Should he pass away during this period, his wife may be entitled to receive all or a percentage of these benefits. Should he be fired, for whatever reason, he may still collect his salary under his contract. A contract is a contract and "golden parachutes" are a part of the system.

So even though the corporation may stall or crash,

the executive is equipped with his "golden parachute" and is thereby guaranteed to land safely and comfortably. He may go to Florida and elsewhere to enjoy a rich retirement life. Who suffers? Who suffers is America: the American economy suffers from this outrageous system.

American Executives Prefer Immediate Rewards

Poverty is very visible all over America, particularly among blacks and Hispanics. The minority issue is a crucial one in America. The gap between rich and poor is enormous. Only one percent of the population controls 36% of the national wealth, an outrageous condition that should somehow be corrected.

A free economy basically should assure profit to anyone who works. Yet if an individual's gains go to the extreme, he becomes a celebrity and an egotist. This is what I have seen to be the case in many corporations today.

Such individuals regard their employees as their own tools to enhance their personal performance for which they collect all the rewards. Should one fail and be fired, he will land comfortably on his feet, thanks to his golden parachute. As an example of an extreme case of such, a friend of mine mismanaged his company while he was its chairman. The company failed, but he and his wife are leading a luxurious life, something that would never happen in Japan. This man has simply played the American game. He had no real intention of remaining with

that company in any case; he was only working to maximize his personal income during that time.

I have been involved in a number of joint venture
projects in America. I make every effort to improve my
joint venture situations. I want to close the deal as
quickly as possible whenever we are involved in substantial capital investment. When we spend capital on facilities investment, we are entitled to tax benefits. I like to
utilize the extra profits generated by these tax benefits
to get rid of debt service. Whenever I suggest that, my
partners ask "why do we have to sacrifice our profits for
people in the future?"

For me, the most critical objective is to make the
company healthy and free of debt service, hoping that
our successors will do the same for their successors by
availing whatever profits we get from repaying the debt,
while my joint venture partners feel that their personal
gains should not be so sacrificed. They have no intention
of remaining with these companies for very long and so
they want to increase their personal income by maximiz-
ing disposable company profits in the short run.

For example, they moved production facilities to Singapore or Japan when the US dollar was high because
they could not expect to maintain high profits when
production costs were high.

This is the case in the semiconductor industry as
well. Production has been moved out of the US, leaving
production primarily with Japan. This has deprived
America of the capacity for anything other than 256 bit
chips. It is cheaper and easier to buy them from Japan,
rather than dealing with expensive, unionized workers

in America. These very same business executives have been blaming the trade imbalance and the Japanese trade surplus for their difficulties while at the same time choosing to import these products from Japan. Japan has not forced them to buy its products, but it cannot begin to catch up on orders placed by American firms.

A Japanese Corporation is a Community Bound Together by a Common Destiny

The fundamental principles which govern a Japanese corporation are basically different from those of an American corporation, from the view-point of both executives and workers.

The structure of pre-war Japanese corporations bears some resemblance to American corporations today to the extent that the president could fire anyone at his discretion. A variety of labor activities were implemented to meet such situations. Taxes were low and executives were leading comfortable lives, able to have company stock allocated, assuring themselves of a comfortable retirement. A top executive was able to buy a house with just one bonus. By the time he retired, he could have several houses for rental, which alone would have ensured a luxurious life.

After the war, General MacArthur changed Japanese labor laws as well as tax laws, among other things, which put Japanese business executives in a different situation. First, they were now unable to fire employees at their discretion, not even to reduce the size of their labor force. At times a company must reduce the size

of the work force if it cannot afford to keep them or
if they are unproductive.

When I first found that American companies can hire
and fire and rehire at will, I wondered perhaps if Japanese companies were more charitable organizations than
profit making institutions. However, Japanese managers
have developed a concept which, in essence binds the
company, workers and management, into a community
with a common fate or destiny. I have explained to
American corporate managers that in Japan, once an
individual is hired, he has been hired for life and unless
he commits some serious offense, the company cannot
fire him. Americans want to know how in the world we
are capable of operating profitably. I say that since a
Japanese company is a community bound together by a
common destiny, like the relationship between a married
couple, all must work together to solve common
problems.

This concept of a fate-sharing community might sound
particular to Japan. However, recently, it appears to
have had some impact on American corporations, which
are showing interest in the Japanese corporate management system. They seem anxious to absorb some of the
positive elements of the Japanese system.

When I find an employee who turns out to be wrong
for a job, I feel it is my fault because I made the decision
to hire him. Generally, I would invest in additional
training, education, or change of duty, even perhaps
sending him overseas for additional experience. As a
result, he will usually turn out to be an asset in the long
run. Even if the positive return is only one out of every

five, that one individual's productivity will cover the losses incurred by the other four. It is a greater loss to lose that one productive person than to maintain the presence of the four incompetents.

In a fate-sharing corporation, one capable individual can easily carry a number of other not-so-capable individuals. The confidence of Japanese employees in their company, knowing that he is employed for life, means that he will develop a strong sense of dedication to that company. For these reasons, Japanese corporate executives are anxious to train their employees well, as they will be their successors.

As the chief executive officer, it is my responsibility not only to pursue profit, but also to create a community where those I have employed can complete their careers 20–30 years from now with the feeling that he had truly made a good life with the company.

Japanese company employees know that they are members of a community bound together by a mutual fate for which they bear the hardships of today in anticipation of a better future. There are many company presidents today in Japan who at one time or another served as union leaders. This fact makes present union leaders feel that they too may, sometime in the future, move into management positions within their company, and therefore their long term interests are closely tied to the company. They do not pursue short term, myopic profits for the immediate future. When the company proposes a plan to save a certain portion of profits for facility investment or to pool for the following year, unions may well be willing to make compromises, because they

know that the future of the workers is tied to the future
of the corporation. I would like to ask presidents of
American corporations if they ever heard of any American union leaders who have become heads of corporations. Japanese executives have a categorically different
corporate philosophy than do American executives, who
are more anxious to demonstrate profitability to please
stockholders. I have asked Americans what, in their
minds, is the meaning of "company." In my mind, it
is a group of people conforming where interests are
shared. I must point out that in the American interpreta-
tion of company, this concept does not exist. It is my
firm conviction that man is created equal, irrespective
of color of skin or nationality and it is natural that
my concept of company includes the employees of my
overseas Sony operations. My California plant opened
in 1972, initially with 250 employees. Soon after the
plant opened, we were hit with the worldwide crisis,
which caused a recession. The California plant was not
immune to this development and the facility lost business
and was unable to support its 250 employees.

The president of Sony America was, of course, an
American and he came to me saying that there was no
other choice but to lay off some of the employees. I
refused his proposal, telling him that I would take the
responsibility for possible losses in order to retain the
employees. We sent capital from the Japanese headquarters to sustain the 250 person work force for some time.
During this period, there was not enough work to keep
everyone busy, so we developed educational programs,
out of which grew not only a sense of appreciation, but

also a real emotional involvement with the company. They began to feel that the plant was their home, and began to clean and polish the facilities, and take care of their work sites on their own. These people became the central core of the California plant, which now employs 1,500 people. They don't even talk about unionizing themselves. American unions are basically industrial, which means that there are always active union leaders from outside who attempted to unionize our plant. Our workers had tee-shirts made, with their own money, saying "WE DON'T NEED THE UNION."

The United Kingdom has a unique law which unionizes every company. Sony UK is no exception. Yet some of our women union members insisted, in an interview on the BBC, that their union is different than other, ordinary ones. This is a positive demonstration of the feeling that we all share the same fate, no matter where we are in the world.

In the U.S. and UK, most employees never have seen their top executives. When I go to one of our plants, I normally mingle with the employees and eat together with them in the company cafeteria. This helps in developing communication and trust. It may be a bit difficult to expect the same response from foreign employees, but it is still the best approach. The Japanese system is not completely applicable to the American system of course. Yet patient demonstration to show that the company truly wishes to protect their interests, even when business is at its worst, will show results. People tend to develop trust under these circumstances. The best thing a company can do is to treat its employees as dignified human beings.

The Japanese Approach Can Be Used Worldwide

European corporations appear to be treating their employees more humanely than their American counterparts, although they are still far from the concept of lifetime employment. Large corporations do not hesitate to lay off employees whenever business is down; they even close operations without notice or sell out, treating employees as if they were tools or equipment.

There is also obvious class discrimination within companies. Engineers, for example, wear white collars, stay in their offices, and seldom show up in the factories. They want to tell workers what to do, rather than donning blues and showing them. In my company, all workers wear the same uniforms. I also wear the same uniform, not only in the plants, but also at company headquarters. All our plant managers do the same. Those who are in training have been instructed to walk through the plant frequently, establishing personal contacts with the workers. Those who become foremen or section managers are encouraged to hold brief meetings each morning with their subordinates to read their mood and detect problems in advance. They are instructed to talk with those who seem ill or depressed, to find out if they need medical care or if they are having family or personal problems. Should this be the case, they should be allowed to take time off and deal with these problems first, while the other workers cover for them. This also helps the sense of togetherness among workers.

On the occasion of 20th and 25th anniversaries of Sony America, my wife and I visited all our American plants, gave talks, had dinner with our employees and shook hands of all our workers. Since at some plants we had three shifts, we had dinner three times in one day, with the night shift taking their turn at 4:00 a.m. I told everyone that we greatly appreciated their contributions which helped make the 25th anniversary a celebration and shook everyone's hand. I was able to feel their responses even physically. These employees told me that this experience was something they never would have had in an American company. I felt our Japanese approach was not foreign to them at all.

One episode made me particularly happy. I visited one of our rather small laboratories, and said I wanted to meet all of its members. The head of the lab asked if he could take my picture. He took his camera from his desk drawer and took me to each member of his staff, introducing me to him or her and taking our picture as we shook hands. There were almost 80 people at this facility and he promised to make a print for each person. I was surprised that this typically Japanese activity was taking place in a facility where there were no Japanese! There again, I felt that we are all basically the same, irrespective of national and cultural differences.

Our style and our efforts have a ripple effect and make other members of our company feel the Sony spirit. I am not saying that whatever style and customs we have developed are automatically good and acceptable everywhere. What I am emphasizing here is that the basic attitude of a corporation and its philosophy can be understood worldwide, and certain aspects of Japanese tradition and style can be rooted overseas.

On the other hand, I recognize fully that certain aspects of American business administration, such as numerical and analytical operations, are excellent as we have sent many individuals from our company to American business schools to learn such matters. Combining good traditions and practices of both the Japanese and American systems will, I believe, make for a very strong corporation.

LET'S BECOME A JAPAN THAT CAN
SAY NO
(MORITA)

*Saying "No" Actually Represents a Deepening
of Mutual Understanding*

It is inevitable that Japanese companies have been establishing American operations. America after the era of Reaganomics is now responding to the trend with new Bush Administration policies. In response, Japan should now begun to make it a habit to say no when its position is clearly negative. It is the rule in the West to say "no" whenever one's position is clearly negative. We are in a business environment where "well" or "probably" have no place in normal business conduct. I have been saying "no" to foreigners for the last thirty years. Clearly, the Japanese Government has missed many, many opportunities to say "no."

Take the auto trade issue, for example. America forced Japan to limit its auto exports to two million units per year under the guise of voluntary restrictions. When the American market became more lucrative, and the number of imported cars could have been increased, American auto manufacturers demanded that the quota be tripled. MITI and the Prime Minister gave into American demands.

In my opinion, this was a great mistake. Both the MITI minister and the prime minister at that time should have taken the position that the American demands were unfair. The Big Three had already increased their profits enormously and individuals such as Lee Iacocca and

Roger Smith were receiving more than a million dollars each in bonuses. They simply demanded special treatment in order to increase profits from the Japanese imports which they sold under their company brands when they requested that the quotas be tripled. That was the time for Japan to have said "you are being hypocritical, criticizing others as unfair when in fact what you are demanding is what is really unfair." The timing was crucial; unless one registers opposition or negative reaction at precisely the right time, Americans take the situation for granted and later insist that they were right as no opposition was registered at the time of the demand. This has always been the case in the past.

The trade imbalance is another case which should be scrutinized as to whether or not American demands are based on fact and reality. I once asked Americans to investigate what Americans had been importing from Japan.

American imports from Japan are mostly products which require a high tech capacity to produce. Many of these products fall into the area of military procurement, but it is true that even the private sector is buying Japanese products which are technologically indispensable. Even some of the inexpensive home electrical appliances may be obtained from Japanese manufacturers within a short time frame if they require high technological skills in the production process.

America has left the production responsibility with Japan, resulting in a heavy dependency upon Japan. American politicians only talk about the results of this situation, blaming Japan for the trade deficit to get votes. Yet it seems that these same politicians don't even know specifically what it is that America buys from Japan. If they took the time and made the effort to seriously investigate the matter, they could not condemn Japan so out of hand.

Japan should tell America that it may buy these quality products irrespective of the exchange rates, even when the US dollar falls to the 100 to 1 ratio. Artificial manipulation of the exchange rate does not benefit the American economy. Such products as transistors, which Sony originally marketed, may today be purchased anywhere outside Japan, and so are not a matter of friction between the US and Japan. Products recently developed in Japan are not as easily obtained elsewhere. There are some things that can only be found in Japan and Japan cannot be blamed for over exposing. Those who say otherwise simply do not know the facts.

Computer terminals are in short supply at present and are being rapidly developed in Japan. Japan should let American know what the situation is and make the US realize that the relationship between the two nations is increasingly mutually dependent.

My purpose in advocating saying "no" is to promote that awareness. "No" is not the beginning of a disagreement or a serious argument. On the contrary, "no" is the beginning of a new collaboration. If Japan truly says "no" when it means "no" it will serve as a means of improving the US–Japan relationship.

National Characteristics Which Make It Difficult for the Japanese to Say "No"

The question arises as to who should say "no?" Japan's Confucian background makes it very difficult for

its people to say "no" within the context of normal
human relationships. In a traditional hierarchy, subordinates dare not say "no" to higher ups without violating
normal courtesy. The higher up takes a "no" from a
subordinate as insubordination. In a staff relationship,
"no" is something to be avoided in order to maintain
smooth human relationships.

Living in a homogeneous society since childhood, we
Japanese have grown up without practical experience in
quarreling and fighting in a heterocultural environment.
Many of us feel that eventually other people will understand our true feelings on an issue without verbalizing
them. In short, we expect a lot when it comes to mutual
understanding. Americans may go directly to their boss
to offer an explanation whenever they feel they are not
properly understood. Japanese, on the other hand, even
if they feel they are not properly understood, remain
hopeful that they will eventually be understood or that
the truth will reveal itself sooner or later. They do the
same with foreigners in foreign countries. They feel that
sincerity and effort should automatically be reciprocated.
In my mind, this can happen only in Japan, but never
in foreign countries. Wordless communication and tele-
pathy will just not happen.

I admit that I may be more westernized than most
Japanese, since I believe that we should be more
straightforward as we become closer, and that a serious
quarrel need not destroy a friendship. This may not be
accepted in a traditional Japanese relationship; we avoid
serious confrontation by turning away from the cold
facts. Instead, we tend to make loose compromises. It

is quite simply our tradition not to say "no" to our friends.

We should not expect to find a similar understanding from foreigners concerning this particular Japanese mentality. It is too easy to expect understanding of one's opposition without using "no." I could say it is a Japanese defect to expect something without using the rational verbal procedures.

If you stay silent when you have a particular demand or an opposing position to express, the other party will take it for granted that you have no demands or opposition. When you close your mind to the outside, remaining in a uniquely Japanese mental framework, you will be isolated in this modern, interdependent world.

LET'S NOT GIVE IN TO AMERICA'S BLUSTER
(ISHIHARA)

Statesmen Ought to Make Best Use of All Available Cards

America has renewed its bluster in the last year. Politicians must sense that they will win more votes bashing Japan than bashing the Soviet Union. Criticism of Japan by U.S. politicians has taken on a rather hysterical tone these days. I experienced it personally when I was there and met with politicians who told me that was a new power shift between the U.S. and U.S.S.R., as if this development should scare Japan somehow. These same politicians indicated that since both Americans and the Soviets are white, at a final confrontation, they might gang up against a non-white Japan.

Japan should never give into such irrational threats. Japan also holds very strong cards in high technology capabilities which is indispensable to military equipment in both the U.S. and U.S.S.R. Yet Japan could well have said "no" to making available specific technology. Japan has substantial national strength to deal with other nations, yet some of the powerful cards it holds have been wasted diplomatically.

I happened to be in America at the time the U.S. Congress passed a resolution to impose sanctions on Japan on the semiconductor issue. Congress seemed to be very excited, almost in the same mood as was the League of Nations was when it sent the Litton Mission to Manchuria to observe Japanese activities there in relation to the Manchukuo Incident.

I talked with members of Congress in this tense atmosphere, and I did not feel they were conducting matters on a rational basis. Some Congressmen were actually brandishing sledgehammers, smashing Toshiba electronic equipment, with their sleeves rolled up. It was just ugly to watch them behave so.

I commented at that time that the U.S. Congress is too hysterical to trust. Their faces turned red in anger and they demanded an explanation. I told them: "Look— only a few decades ago you passed the Prohibition Amendment. No sincere Congress would ever pass such irrational legislation." They all just grinned at me in response.

Yet I must admit, that it was Japan who aggravated the semiconductor issue to such a low level, by not saying "no" on the appropriate occasions.

After he was elected to a second term, Mr. Nakasone promised America that Japan would avail highly strategic technology without giving adequate thought to the significance of that kind of commitment. The strongest card, which he should have played, was virtually given away free to America. He probably wanted to impress America, hoping for a tacit reciprocity from a thankful U.S. Unfortunately, it was only Mr. Nakasone who recognized the value of that card at the time. Both the Liberal Democrats and opposition parties overlooked the significance of this issue. I assume that the leaders of those parties, such as Takeshita, Miyazawa and Abe did not know it either. It is such a pity that Japan's politicians are not aware of the political significance of Japan's high technology capabilities.

In reality, Japanese technology has advanced so much that America gets hysterical, an indication that tremendous value of that card—perhaps our ace. My frustration stems from the fact that Japan has not, so far, utilized that powerful card in the arena of international relations.

What Mr. Nakasone got out of the free gift was Reagan's friendship, so-called. We all know that love and friendship alone cannot solve international conflicts and hardships.

Nakasone Bungled the Relationship

I truly regret that Japanese diplomacy has been based on a series of "yeses" instead of skillful manipulation of strong ace cards. Former prime minister Nakasone has done a substantial disservice to Japan in terms of his handling of relations with the U.S. These are among his most unfortunate mistakes. He boasted of the so-called "Ron-Yasu" relationship as if he had succeeded in bringing about a skillful policy toward the U.S. In reality, he was simply a lowly yesman to Reagan.

It was actually I who introduced Mr. Nakasone to Mr. Reagan. I asked one of Mr. Reagan's assistants if he ever recalled a "no" from Nakasone to Reagan. He immediately replied he did not know of any, and Mr. Nakasone was a "nice guy with a sardonic smile."

Former Prime Minister Nakasone was in a position to know that Japan's leading edge technology was superior to that of the U.S. so much so that Americans had become nervous concerning the magnitude of Japan's superiority in the area. Yet he still did not say "no." Was he taken advantage of? Did he have some weak spot as did the prime minister (Tanaka) at the time of the Lockheed scandal during the Nixon Administration? Otherwise, Japanese leaders who hold such high cards should be able to play them in dealing with American demands.

The FSX, the next generation of fighters, developed by Mitsubishi Heavy Industries during the Nakasone era, has become another source of controversy in the U.S. as it relates to defense matters. Further development of the FSX appears to be quashed by the U.S. I am unaware of any deals made under the table, but there is considerable frustration in Japan over the matter.

Mitsubishi Heavy Industries is a conglomerate with a wide variety of technology used in manufacturing advanced products. The chief engineer there is a contemporary of mine who developed the most advanced land-to-air missile. He is also the man responsible for the design of the next generation fighter and he believes that Japan should have its own capacity to provide such equipment, which of course astonishes Americans.

The FSX is a marvelous and formidable fighter. No existing fighter, including the F-15 and the F-16 can match it in a dog fight. I recall when the Secretary of Defense Weinberger became serious about quashing the FSX Japanese development plan, strictly out of fear.

Unfortunately, Japan has not yet developed a powerful enough jet engine, although I advocated such development while I was a member of the Upper House. Japan still must purchase jet engines, which are mounted on the F-15 and F-16. If America gets really nasty, Japan could buy engines from France, which is quite anxious to export military equipment (at the same time that country's president is advocating truces all over the world, I might add). If France is reluctant to sell what we need, I would not mind going to the Soviet Union, although the quality of the Russian engines is not particularly impressive.

New Mitsubishi designed jet fighters equipped with Russian engines may only have a top speed of 95% of existing F-15 and F-16 class fighters, so one might think them inferior. On the contrary, their combat capability is far superior in a dog-fight situation. It can make a 380 degree turn with a third of the diameter needed by other top fighters. The F15 and 16 require 5000 meters; the Mitsubishi fighter only requires 1600 meters. Just think of war a game of tag. What is necessary is not maximum speed but great maneuverability. Mistubishi's FSX fighter can get right on an enemy plane and send heat-seeking missiles with 100% accuracy. Incidently, there are two types of air-to-air missiles, heat seeking and radar controlled. The radar controlled type may even fail to hit a jumbo jet, while the heat tracing type can fine tune its direction to head for the enemy's source of heat.

The FSX was a surprise to the Americans, as were the Zero fighters at the beginning of the Second World War. They never expected to see such an advanced fighter as the Zero, which virtually controlled the air at the beginning of the war. That such a formidable weapon as the FSX is in production today outside the US came as shock to Americans. The Japanese FSX is equipped with four vertical fins, similar to shark's fins. Each acts as a steering mechanism, like the steering wheel of a four wheel drive automobile that can make a complete turn in a small area without moving back and forth. Such a marvelous idea probably is not the monopoly of Japan, but it was a Japanese manufacturer who developed the idea into reality, thanks to Japanese advanced high technology.

Russian fighters are also equipped using Japanese know-how, especially in the areas of ceramics and carbon fibers. Special paints on American reconnaissance planes which assist in avoiding radar detection are also made in Japan.

Shocked by the high standards of the FSX, I guess that the US pressured Mr. Nakasone, probably citing his earlier commitment on technology. His submission to American pressure eventually caused the mothballing of the FSX to be replaced by future projects of a joint US–Japan development plan. In November 1988, the two governments signed an agreement that set the course for the joint development of the FSX; an agreement which leaves many unsolved problems at the industry level.

One of the manufacturers involved, General Dynamics, was very anxious to assume the initiative on the project, dividing it up among others. It met with resistance from Mitsubishi, and General Dynamics came up with a plan that would separate the development of the left and right wing—a very peculiar approach.

In short, America wants to steal Japanese know-how.

They cannot manufacture the most technologically advanced fighters without advanced ceramic and carbon fiber technology from Japan. That is why America is applying so much pressure, attempting to force Japan to come to American terms. Some of Japan's industry representatives appear willing to deal with the Americans under the table, probably with the good intentions of smoothing US–Japan relations on the issue. I happen to disagree with such an approach. We just cannot give in on this issue. We must be persistent to the maximum degree. If America does not appreciate a rational division of labor on the project, we should discontinue the project and start all over from scratch.

The joint development idea is a legacy of the Reagan–Nakasone era. Both men are now out of power and we can retract the whole thing and tell the US that we have decided to develop our own project without its participation. It is our choice. We must bluff to counter American bluff, otherwise we will continue to be the loser.

I brought this subject up the other day to Mr. Nakasone. He responded: "Well you had a pretty sharp interest in that issue at the time." I said that I was "probably the only one concerned about the issue at the time." Mr. Nakasone then insisted that he made the decision to compromise in order to maintain good US–Japan relations. He also admitted that America was then already very much afraid of further Japanese technological advances. Well, compromise is fine, but in reality this was not a compromise: it was a sell-out—a simple sell-out of Japan's interests.

I don't regret it any less when we make the silly mistake of not saying "no" especially when we hold the strong cards. Such freebies are now taken for granted and America comes back with more bluff. On the record, USTR Yeutter stated that the "application of high pressure is the best way to manipulate Japan."

My position may draw some criticism in Japan, where it probably will be said that I am playing with dynamite in dealing with America in this fashion. It goes without saying that an equal partnership must be carried out without humiliating pressure or compromise as the result of such pressure. This is the reason I am advocating that Japan say "no." "No" is an important instrument in the bargaining process.

Diplomacy should be Free of External Pressures

Diplomacy which lacks the "no" factor cannot be diplomacy for the benefit of Japan. Japan has had a solid basis for saying "no" on many occasions. All we must do is play our cards wisely, playing our ace intelligently. Japan is very poor at diplomatic tactics. It is a wonder to me that Japan has failed to recognize that its initiatives are instrumental in the ultimate decision making process in the international arena.

Mr. Glen Fukushima, an American of Japanese descent in the office of the USTR (Deputy Assistant USTR for Japan and China), who was acquainted with Senator Aquino of the Philippines while both were at Harvard, is one of the most capable Asian specialists. His wife is an intellectual Keio University graduate, who prefers to live in Japan, forcing Glen to commute to Japan two or three times a month.

On one occasion, I had dinner with him and asked him what America's next Japan-bashing scenario would entail. He replied that the US would take up the distribution issue since this cannot be rectified by Japanese politicians without pressure from the US. I hate to use American pressure in order to accomplish a national objective, yet, I must admit that the distribution system is one of Japan's biggest headaches today. There is no question that high prices in Japan are caused by the distribution system itself, which is made worse by Japanese politicians.

There are domestic areas where we Japanese must say "no" also, even before we say "no" to outsiders. The liberalization of rice is one such issue. Opinions on the rice issue sharply divide politicians such as I, whose constituents are urban, from those representing farmers.

Former minister of agriculture Sato is a good friend of mine, but his advocacy of food security is becoming diminished. Inevitably, mutual dependence is becoming more and more a reality in our world today. America was not even able to place a ban on exports of grain to the Soviet Union when the Russians invaded Afghanistan. There would have been too much pressure from American farmers. If that is the case, it would probably be practically impossible to put a ban on agricultural exports to Japan. The rice issue has its sentimental aspects in Japan as well as its practical aspects, which make the overall issue more complicated. Yet it is obvious that we must liberalize the market. Such is also true of construction projects. It is inevitable that we allow foreign construction firms to participate in Japanese public construction projects. Japanese general contractors have been maintaining prices as much as 40% higher in comparison to foreign bidders, due to bid rigging traditions to assure a monopoly on business for themselves. There is no way these practices could ever be free of foreign criticism.

In the course of my conversation with Glen Fukushima, I asked whom among the Japanese negotiators he considers the best. He, immediately came up with the name of MITI's Kuroda, whom the Japanese press used to criticize for his tough positions. The press claimed that his participation aggravated the problem with the US. The Americans criticized him for being stubborn. Strangely, the American negotiator named him the most effective. He is stubborn and is able to say "no" decisively whenever he should do so. The Americans usually try to overpower negotiations by increasing pressure. But Kuroda does not feel that he must say "yes" to American pressure. America is a giant in many ways and, in many ways, Japan is a dwarf. This obvious contrast has been exploited by the Americans often in the past. Mr. Kuroda kept pointing out that irrational pressure is not the result of reason or logic, and reinforced this position by withstanding increasing pressure. His "no" is not a no for its own sake; he always states his reasons. This is the proper approach and attitude in negotiations. In the past, there have been allegations that Japanese logic and opinions have not made any sense to the other side.

When the opposing side points out that Japanese opinions and demands have no logical basis, all of a sudden
the illogical Japanese start saying "yes, yes, yes" in a
panic. But these "yeses" do not necessarily mean yes
in the sense of positive assertion. At any rate, the other
side then comes to the conclusion that Japan will not
take action unless pressure is placed on them. This is
a rather unfortunate situation for the people of Japan.
The Japanese image of being soft in the face of pressure
does not help Japan's diplomatic efforts at all.

I have often suggested that at least half of Japan's
diplomats stationed abroad be civilians. Those who are
in business and other professions who have dealt with
foreigners are in a better position to represent the interests of Japan than are career diplomats. Send Mr. Morita
to America as our ambassador: a brilliant idea! But it
should not be just an idea. I truly believe that it would
be most beneficial to the US–Japan relationship to have
such an ambassador from Japan to the US.

THE U.S. AND JAPAN ARE "INESCAPABLY INTERDEPENDENT"
(MORITA)

No Way To Avoid the Trade Frictions

Recently the expression, "inescapable interdependence" has been heard quite often among Americans. If we dare to explain this concept in a more extreme way, perhaps we can say it's a "fatal attraction". With this trend now prevailing in the world, we have no choice but to live cooperatively. Everyone on earth not just the United States and Japan is mutually dependent and this is unavoidable. This is the times that we are facing now. What does cooperation mean?

A Japanese tends to say, "Let's work together." But I often wonder whether they really understand its meaning. This can be applicable to Americans, as well. We are at home using this expression but it seems to only be used as a convenience. Furthermore it is out of the question to force "cooperation" through threats.

To cooperate is to maintain harmony. It is not harmonious to force your adversary. When they cope with you, you, too, must cope with them. You have to give up some of your interest; you must abandon something.

I tell people whenever I have a chance that we know what it is to be selfish but hardly anybody is aware when he himself is being selfish. We say that one is selfish but actually this person probably has no idea that he is perceived as such. In this sense, Japan also can be thought a little bit selfish by other countries, although we hardly have such idea.

Looking for the reason, we are so perceived, the opening of the domestic market can be one example. Everyone agrees that we should open our markets to foreign traders, but when it comes to individual, this is hard to actualize since someone says, "no, I cannot accept this", and then someone else says, "no, I cannot accept that." Although at summit meetings, Japanese leaders assure others that they will do their best, and they actually do try to open the market. In the end, however, this is never actualized since their promise goes against domestic interest groups and they are forced to back down. Only lip-serve followed by no achievement might result in being called "liars" and this is surely worse than "selfish."

The development of communication technologies means this is a shrinking world and any country will be left alone if it does not talk frankly to its people and friendly countries about the compromises that they must accept.

Free people in the free world ask for their freedom but at the same time they respect the freedom of others. And I think it is genuine freedom to think "we should abandon some so that we can respect others". It will simply increase friction if we just look out for our own benefit, and put priority on winning the race based on the premise that we simply can focus on our interests alone since we are in the world of free economy.

We should also recognize that friction seldom occurs with those who are far from you. Friction occurs as we move close. We cannot escape from the trade friction

as long as we belong to the world of "inescapable interdependence".

Japan's Central Role in Asia

The closer we become, the harsher the friction can
be. So it would be wise for us to prepare for problems
with neighboring Asian countries.

I went to Singapore recently to attend a ceremony
marking the opening of our new plant, and had a chance
to talk with President Lee Kuan Yew who has been a
friend for a long time. He invited me to his home, we
talked over the dinner and I stayed with him.

The plant our company opened this time in Singapore
is operated automatically by robots. We use materials
Singapore supplies and employ able engineers graduated
from good schools in Singapore, producing special parts
in large numbers. The plant itself will be a foothold to
supply the products all over the world. When I proudly
held forth my new plant, he was very pleased and said
that in the past when Japanese firms opened plants in
his country, they needed a large number of employees,
where they in fact have never had enough personnel.
Because of the nature of his country, that is, Singapore
is a small island, this caused wage increases at a drastic
pace. This is what they had wanted; a plant with sophisti-
cated technology.

Transferring our technologies, not teaching management, I believe, the best way to alleviate friction between Southeast Asian countries and Japan. These countries, NICS, then NIES, are now the Four Tigers or Five

Tigers. It might be too much to say that they developed thanks to the Japanese economy and industrial technologies, but I believe we contributed to them in such a way that contributed to their current prosperity. From now on, Japan will need to take a major role in Asia. You already are able to see this is happening when you recognize that Tokyo has taken a major role as a finance and money center like New York and London.

In the past, we yearned to go to New York when we were young. Similarly, the youth of Southeast Asia yearn and to visit Tokyo or Disneyland in Japan. I should avoid the expression, "leadership", but Japan has begun to assume that role as a center in Asia.

To take on the role as an initiator means we must also be able to take on the role of arbitrator. That is, we must think carefully what constitutes a real leadership role in this mutually dependent world.

America, You Had Better Give Up Certain Arrogance

As you (Mr. Ishihara) mentioned before, rapprochement between the United States and the Soviet Union and Japan's involvement in their military strategies because of its highly-sophisticated technology directly affects new trends on the world scene.

I do not think anybody imagined a decade ago that these two superpowers would be mutually dependent on each other in a military sense and that there would be a strange structure in the power balance among the United States, the Soviet Union and Japan. Nobody can deny that we are going to have a totally new configuration in the balance of power in the world.

Facing this, most important to Japan in the practical sense, is the relationship between Japan and the United States. Japan needs the United States. I think the United States needs Japan as well. It is a bond we can never cut, and this might be the "fatal attraction" between us. Since we can never separate, we had better look for the way to develop through cooperation a healthy relationship through cooperation. And we want to ask you Americans, "what is going on now in your country? Do Americans really understand the meaning of 'freedom' and the role of Japan which is so necessary to the United States?" When you see present conditions, it is obvious that the United States is not strong enough in a fundamental and structural sense. So, I think what is most important is that we ask them frankly as an equal and not as a subordinate, "Are you really sure that you are all right?" We will be in trouble as will the whole world if the United States is not strong enough in the fundamentals and this means more than talking about something current. It must be recognized by Mr. Bush as well. In this sense, it is important for Mr. Takeshita to deliver our message correctly in the coming summit. In my understanding, however, these summit meetings are held according to an itinerary prepared at the working level and they decided what was supposed to be said by the leaders. In negotiations among business leaders, we, top management hold discussions face to face, saying "yes" or "no", or "if you will do that, we will do this." However, we have a tendency to prepare answers for negotiations even in business world in Japan. Take my case, for example. Once a chairman of a large Japanese firm was visiting me and I planned to talk with him face to face. Then, someone from that office called us and asked what I was going to talk about when we met. "Our chairman is going to say such and such. How will you respond?" They wanted to prepare all answers beforehand. I do not think we need to have meetings if the content is planned beforehand. I want Mr. Takeshita to say correctly how we, Japanese, see the present situation in the United States and tell them clearly what we want them to do. I think we should tell them, "please do not cling to the image that you are the superpower, but rather look for the way to get your economy on the road to recovery. We should tell them, "we are going to back up your dollar, so face the fact and issue yenbonds, for example, as Carter Administration issued pound-bonds." Americans have to abandon the idea, such as "our federal obligations do not bother us since we can print more green backs." They have to change the way they think about their own economy. To this end, we Japanese must deliver the message "if you cannot make both ends meet, we cannot either." We must do this even if it takes time to make them understand.

It is high time to let them know we might go bankrupt together if things are not resolved. The United States and Japan relationship is in serious trouble. Because of our historical discipline, Japan has adhered to the principle that "silence is golden", but I believe that Japan must insist that the United States do what must be done.

An outspoken person like me is easily criticized from every corner and I am sure Mr. Ishihara has had the same experience since he is also very outspoken. But to be silent and to put up with things do not work at all in the West. As Ishihara has suggested, I think we should say what we have to say. If not, I am afraid that we will lose our own identity as Japanese in the world.

JAPAN SHOULD LIVE IN HARMONY
WITH ASIA
(ISHIHARA)

Restrain America!

When the time comes when Japan does say "no" decisively on a particular issue, there may be a dramatic reaction. It should come as a shock to the Americans, and a number of different reactions would be possible. Even now, some Americans suggest the possible physical occupation of Japan in case Japan engages in semiconductor trade with the Soviet Union.

Yet when the time comes, we may well dare to say "no." The relationship between Japan and the U.S., as Mr. Morita describes it is unbreakable. However, the whole world does not exist for the sake of Japan and the U.S. Japan's relationship with the rest of the world does not exist only in relation to or through the U.S. Should America behave unreasonably toward Japan, Japan must open channels to deal with the rest of the world from a different standpoint than on the basis of the U.S.–Japan relationship and is must show that it is doing this to the Americans.

America itself has already exhibited certain indications that it is shifting towards a closer relationship with the Soviet Union, as Alvin Toffler stated, insinuating that Japan will be threatened once the U.S. establishes a more collaborative relationship with the Soviet Union similar to the case of the U.S. movement toward China, which it did without keeping Japan advised. Beyond the shock of American's new relationship with China, which burst forth in December 1978, there was also an astonishing high technology demonstration.

I for one had a chance to observe some of that demonstration. It began with a set of satellite photos which Dr. Kissinger brought to China. At the time, Viet Nam was engaged in a military conflict with China, subsequent to the fall of the Saigon government in April 1970 and the Cambodian war. The Sino-Vietnamese war was recklessly provoked by Deng Shao Ping, chief of staff in China. In the initial encounters, China was severely defeated. The real power behind Viet Nam was the Soviet Union. The Soviet Union provided Viet Nam with detailed satellite photos illustrating the movements of the Chinese military, the number of soldiers and divisions, the number of tanks unloaded at Kuang Tong station and which direction all these troops took. Taking advantage of the superior information available to them, as provided by the Soviet Union, Viet Nam was able to lure Chinese troops deep into the mountains, then destroyed them with anti-tank missiles. This miserable battle was all recorded by American satellites, which Dr. Kissinger presented to the Chinese with the comment "what a silly war you people have conducted."

Needless to say, it was a shock to the Chinese leaders to see how, step by step their military was demolished.

I assume that the Americans showed another series of satellite pictures showing the horrible massacre of Chinese soldiers at the siege of Damansky Island (in Russian, or Chin Pao Island (in Chinese), which is located in the middle of the Amur (phonetic rendering) River. At first, only a small number of Russian soldiers occu-

pied the island and they were soon driven off by the
Chinese, who had many more troops than did the Russians. The Russians returned in greater numbers and
recaptured the island. Finally, the Chinese sent the
equivalent of a human wave of troops, almost flooding
the island with soldiers. As the Chinese shouted victory,
the island was surrounded by a sudden mist and eventually it was covered by a dense fog. The Russians exploited this climatic assistance, surrounding the island
with tanks and opening a salvo. At dawn, there were
a great many dead Chinese troops. The Russians landed
their tanks, rolling over the dead, wounded, and living,
reducing all to nothing.

The Americans showed clear pictures of the events,
illustrating what had taken place using satellite pictures,
a great demonstration of the combination of technology
and intelligence gathering. China was shocked and dis-
turbed that it could not effectively counter a situation
like that as they simply did not have access to the
technology required. They listened to the Americans,
and agreed to the development of a bilateral relationship
with the U.S. on American terms. America had played
its high tech card quite effectively.

The normalization of relations with China, by-passing
Japan, set a precedent and provided a basis for other
such threats to Japan by the U.S. America can bluff
Japan by indicating that it can develop a similar relation-
ship with the Soviet Union, without consultation, so that
Japan would be less needed within the framework of
U.S. global strategy. But Japan has a similar card to
play, to counter the American bluff.

Some of Japan's business leaders have long had an

interest in Siberian development, which now appears to be a realistic possibility. Some of them are of the opinion that Japan could go neutral, revoking the U.S.–Japan Security Treaty, if the Soviets will return the northern islands, granted that Japan would be given the right to develop Siberian resources.

This may be a realistic choice from the Soviet point of view since some critical technologies such as linear technology are available from Japan. The U.S. simply does not have them. Japan had better start sending some signals of its own to America. My American friends comment that my behavior in the U.S. is too provocative; I feel that more of us should speak out like this more often.

Japan could have the Soviets formally request Japan's linear technology. The COCOM would claim that it is illegal for Japan to provide this technology. Japan would then amount a public relations campaign, appealing to the rest of the world that the use of its linear technology is simply to enhance the efficiency of the Soviet railroad system in Siberia so that travel time is shortened and the whole thing will be rationalized as an attempt to restrain American intervention. In fact, the UK and France are champions at this kind of public relations game, in combination with diplomacy. We need more skillful players in the game to counter the formidable American challenges in the international arena.

Japan Is Not Getting a Free Ride on the U.S.–Japan Security Pact

It goes without saying that the U.S.–Japan relationship is a vital one. The security treaty has certainly been helpful to Japan. America, however, has chosen to become involved for American interests; it did not want to see the restoration of Japanese military power. However, the so-called American nuclear umbrella as a deterrent power for Japan is not as valuable as the Americans have said. I verified this myself twenty years ago and put it into the official record. The American nuclear umbrella is just an illusion as far as the Japanese people are concerned. Also, the so-called "free ride" on the U.S.–Japan Security treaty is no such thing and has no earthly basis. I have stated this repeatedly. The Japanese people have been forced to thank the U.S. for an illusion. Both the U.S. and the USSR had to enter into the INF agreement due to the nature of a changing power shift in the world, which on the bottom line, is inevitable in light of the high technology dominance by Japan. This has been clearly seen by individuals such as Dr. Kissinger, who even foresaw the situation today long ago, a position he has stated on a number of occasions. Poor Japanese politicians have never studied these issues systematically and therefore can never provide a rebuttal to American allegations. Americans, for their part, seem to have emotional and intellectual difficulties in admitting to changes and new developments.

A Pentagon task force sent a warning on electronics, with particular emphasis on semiconductors, those who have nothing to worry about but Japan. America is very seriously concerned about losing power of any kind to Japan. Some Americans have been raising their voices in advocation of an increased Japanese defense capacity. This may be a worthwhile suggestion. We should overhaul our current defense system, although I am not advocating an abrupt cutting of ties with the U.S. We have accepted this absurd defense formula consisting of three defense forces. This system must be completely overhauled to suit present realities, including a much greater deterrent capacity, exploiting our high technology to the maximum. We should develop the most persuasive and demonstrable deterrent formula which would, without any doubt, show our adversaries that any attack on Japan will end with unbearable damage to the aggressor from both a strategic and a tactical viewpoint.

Production and maintenance of escort ships which can only exhaust their missiles and ammunition within a few minutes, and then sit and wait for death is absurd. Participation in RIMPAC with such equipment makes no sense. RIMPAC has nothing to do with the concept of active defense.

In a lecture that the Defense College of Japan, the commander of the US 7th Fleet declared that it is 100% unlikely that Soviet forces could land on Japanese territory. This is honest- but stupid-comment. Some time ago, we invited a famous Israeli tank division commander named Tam (phonetic rendering) to Japan. He kept annoying the Defense Agency by asking why Japan was building tanks. He was considered to be one of the top tank strategists in the world, and he told us that even on Hokkaido there was no need of tanks for defense. He said that Soviet attacks would have to be destroyed at sea. He also expressed doubt in the value of escort ships.

His points are absolutely valid. Tanks and escort ships

were built and maintained at the direction of the Americans. America has imposed its defense formula for Japan on Japan, reproducing its own defense formula within Japan. Thus, Japan has ended up with the defense system it has simply because of one-sided, pro-American diplomacy: one in which Japan says only "yes."

I conducted my own cost analysis of Japanese defense systems and discovered the whole thing could be far less expensive if Japan developed its own system in accordance with its own initiatives and planning, in comparison to the expenditures forced on us today by the US. Despite the bowing under to American will by Japan, it still is the target of American politicians such as McClosky who charge that "Japan is protected by American blood shed in the Persian Gulf."

The time has come for Japan to tell the US that we do not need American protection. Japan will protect itself with its own power and wisdom. This will require a strong commitment and will on our part. We can do it as long as there is a national consensus to do so. There may be some political difficulties at this point in forming this consensus. From both a financial and a technological point of view, there are no barriers to accomplishing this goal in the near future. We can develop a more effective and efficient defense capability at less than we are paying today.

In reality, the abrupt cancellation of the security treaty is not feasible. But it is a diplomatic option and a powerful card. Outright refusal to consider such an option means giving up a valuable diplomatic card. The fact remains that we do not necessarily need the security treaty and a security system which will meet Japanese needs, can be build by Japan alone.

Both the right and left on this issue tend to become fanatical on the security treaty debate. It is most regrettable that we do not have a cool and rational forum where the objective profit and loss aspects of the issue can be analyzed. But the time will come when we will have to face this issue and this time is in the near future.

The current state of the Liberal Democratic Party means that it cannot afford a serious deliberation on this issue. Once the opposition parties disassociate themselves from a one-sided pro Russian and Chinese policy and demonstrate their capacity to be able to replace the LDP as alternative political parties fully recognized by the voters, we will be in the position to examine our options with greater flexibility.

Japan Should Live in Harmony With Asia

Japanese popular songs are heard all over Asia these days; it reminds me of the time when the Japanese became so interested in American pop music, which, at the time, conditioned our psycho-emotional base so that post-war Japan evolved into a consumer-oriented society. Structurally, there must be similar powers during such social phenomena and I wonder what it is today.

As a matter of fact, it has always been some technological breakthrough which has moved history into the next stage, during any given era, even as far back as the stone age or the copper epoch. Technology has always set the pace of civilization and cultures flourish on this basis. When we start seeing only the pretty flowers that are the result of this flourishing and forget about the roots that nourish the blossoms, we soon experience the decline of the civilization, as has been the case of nations in the past. This is the way I interpret history, in cool and orthodox terms.

With respect to the development of the commercial uses of the semiconductor, materialized by Japan in Asia, I must say that we can easily understand the reason why this happened. When the French Minister of Culture, Andre Malroux, came to Japan, he pointed out the distinction between Western religious artifacts and those of Japan. He told an audience that the Western expression of a crucified Christ is bloody and even grotesque and might well discourage a religious attachment to Christ. However, he said, the Miroku Buddha at the Horiyuji Temple emits such a sublime beauty, beyond the barriers of race and religion, that it is raised to the level of an eternal or ultimate object to be revered.

What he meant was that the type of beauty and the impression given in such an artifact as the Miroku Buddha or the Horiyuji Temple attracts interest and respect from all over the world, beyond national, racial, and cultural boundaries. These are products of refinement from Japanese people. The original image of Buddha came from India, by way of China and the Korean peninsula. The image of Buddha in Japan is the product of the refinement of Japanese art. The process has been constantly refined and it becomes a product of Japanese intellectual processes, as the Minister explained, it is clearly Japanese.

In my judgment, Japan has acquired this ability primarily because of the particular geographical environment surrounding the Japanese archipelago. In the long journey from West to East, Japan is located at a dead end; there is nothing beyond except the Pacific Ocean. Japan is in no position to pass on to any other nations what it has received; it must live with what it receives for the rest of history. Everything stops at Japan; the Japanese people refine what has come their way; Japan is the last stop in cultural transition.

Among Japanese statesmen, Mr. Minora Genda is one I truly respect. He once said that Western swords were basically instruments of killing, although there are some variations, such as those used in the sport of fencing. But these swords are just tools and we cannot be impressed looking as Western swords. Japanese swords make viewers feel they are looking at artifacts and that they are being invited in the world of art and mystery. He went on to say that the Japanese people have converted these awful tools, made originally to butcher other people, into art objects.

Another time, Mr. Genda told me: "Mr. Ishihara— after all, in the end, Japan will be all right. It is able to defend itself." When I replied, "how," he said that "Japan's technology can be the basis of Japan's defense." What he had pointed out was that Japanese technology, which has been refined and polished to the ultimate extent, just like the swords, would provide the basis for Japan future existence.

Mr. Genda also affirmed the points I made, suggesting that in certain crucial technological areas, Japan should move at least five years ahead of other nations and if possible, further, to at least ten years. As long as Japan maintains that ten year advance, it will be in a safe position for the first twenty-five years of the 21st century. And this can be accomplished if politicians use their ace cards wisely.

I had an argument with an American correspondent recently. I asked him to look at those developing nations which were under American auspices. The Philippines and those in Africa, Central and South America are all in hopeless situations. Americans once called the Philippines "a showcase of democracy." I said that Americans are mistaken.

While the Philippines may have felt more comfortable under American administration than under Spanish colonial rule, and while they still listen to America, the US have never really imparted to them an understanding of genuine democracy. The chairman of the House Subcommittee on Southeast Asia once suggested to me that the US and Japan should split the cost of financial aid to the Philippines. I responded: "You're kidding!" He said that money alone cannot improve the situation in the Philippines because of the internal situation. The US does not even know where its aid money actually ends up. And most fundamentally, social conflict in a nation cannot be solved with an outsider's cash.

The most crucial task in the Philippines is to face the cause of social turmoil there. The cause is the role of the landowners; Philippine landowners have accumulated incredible power and wealth, syphoning everything from the ordinary people. These landowners will get no sympathy from me. The Philippines must act to redistribute the land and wealth in much the same manner as took place in Japan after the war. Landowners cannot remain landowners unless the country is stabilized. Should a military junta take power, and decide upon a socialist economic policy, these landowners would be wiped out.

Usurpers must be removed, otherwise there is no way the seeds of democracy can be planted. This so-called "showcase of democracy" is empty. And pouring additional aid money into the hands of the landowners on the form of compensation for losing their land is not only a utter waste of funds, but also ruins any basis for self-help and self-motivation.

There is a chieftain in the Truk Islands, who speaks Japanese, and who said that since the Japanese left, their children have only learned to be lazy as the Americans give aid—money and things which spoil human beings. If you give people lettuce seeds, he said, they will learn to grow lettuce, but if you give them money they will simply import lettuce and learn nothing.

America is reluctant to recognize the importance and value of local cultures. Christian missionaries do not permit the natives to chant their charms and they prohibit the use of herbs as medicine—herbs that have traditionally been used in healing sicknesses, found in certain localities and used according to local customs. Local festivals are banned, so that traditional songs and dances are forgotten. Tradition is dismantled. Americans force other cultures to give up their traditional value and impose the American culture upon them. And they do not even recognize that this is an atrocity—a barbaric act!

Natives who once has a traditional festival similar to Japan's ceremony of tasting the fruits of the first harvest. (Our ancestors may well have come from these southern islands, by the way). The festival was held on the night of the full moon. Beating drums and dancing, the people indulged in open sex as the festival had by its nature this element of fertility. Christian priests prohibited these festivals and instructed the natives to bring the fruits of the harvest to the church altar. One hour after this was done, the priests ate the gifts. The chieftain, still speaking Japanese, complained "we did not grow this to feed priests." This kind of misunderstanding goes on and on and Americans don't even realize it.

Those Asian nations where the economy has been a success story, such as Korea, Taiwan, and Singapore, were all, at one time or another, under Japanese administration. We are aware that some negative things happened under the Japanese administration, but it cannot be denied that many positive changes were left behind.

Among the resource supplying nations, the only Southeast Asian nations which have developed stable socio-economic systems are those where Japan has cooperated as a fellow Asian country. I pointed this out to that correspondent with whom I had the argument; in return he only kept silent.

In any case, these NICS are turning into NIES who are catching up to Japan, which makes Japan nervous. However, this is fine with me. Japan should work more positively, basing its approach on the premise that we must live in harmony with other Asian nations, developing constructive political strategies to assist these countries economically and politically. Entering a new era—the Pacific Age-Japan cannot remain prosperous without the rest of Asia. We need Asia more than we need America.

Japan Can be Admitted to the World Community by Saying "No."

Japan is not quite the tiny country most Japanese think it is. We should not be presumptuous or arrogant, ending up hated by others, but should have pride and dignity as respected members of the world community.

Our world view appears to be very peculiar, conditioned in part by our geography and our climate. In our mind, Japan and the rest of the world do not exist in a concentric circle. The rest of the world has its center and the center of Japan is somewhere outside this. I feel it is time to overhaul this concept and enter into the concentric world.

We want to enter that arena not through the kind of individual performance as given by Mr. Nakasone, but rather by saying "no" decisively. The Japanese people will define their position in facing the consequences and significance of their "no" and will be able to join the world community in the concentric circle as a truly "adult" member. It is therefore imperative to normalize our relationship with the US, so we can get on with becoming a true member of the world community.

I often suggested a G2 conference with the US. This

would help establish Japan's status and America might well welcome the suggestion. When there are only two parties meeting, Japan will have no choice but to say "yes" or "no" without resorting to gray areas. Japan must be equipped with logic and reason whenever it says "no." Best of all, by holding a G2, Japan will have only itself and the US with which to be concerned, making it easier to stick to the "no." No other nation will pay attention to Japan if Japan cannot say "no" to the US. A good example is China.

Japan is flattered by many nations these days for no other reason than its wealth. Money is important, but Japan has many more valuable assets, such as tradition, culture, creativity, as well as powerful high technology; this last item is one that even the US and USSR cannot afford to ignore. In order to make the rest of the world realize that Japan has much more to offer than wealth, we must develop the logic and reasoning to be able to say "no," explain why, and stick to it at certain crucial moments.